PENGUIN BOOKS

THE HEART OF THE HUNTER

Laurens van der Post was born in Africa in 1906. Most of his adult life has been spent with one foot there and one in England. His professions of writer and farmer were interrupted by ten years of soldiering – behind enemy lines in Abyssinia, and also in the Western Desert and the Far East, where he was taken prisoner by the Japanese while commanding a small guerrilla unit. He went straight from prison back to active service in Java, served on Lord Mountbatten's staff and, when the British forces withdrew from Java, remained behind as Military Attaché to the British Minister. Since 1949 he has undertaken several official missions exploring little-known parts of Africa. His independent expedition to the Kalahari Desert in search of the Bushmen was the subject of his famous documentary film and of *The Lost World of the Kalahari* (published in Penguins). His other books include *Venture to the Interior* (published in Penguins), *The Face Beside the Fire* (1953), *Flamingo Feather* (1955), *The Dark Eye in Africa* (1955), *The Seed and the Sower* (1963), *Journey into Russia* (1964), *The Hunter and the Whale* (1967) and *A Portrait of Japan* (1968). His latest book is *A Story Like the Wind* (1972). Colonel van der Post, who is married, was awarded the C.B.E. for his services in the field.

The Heart of the Hunter

Laurens van der Post

with drawings by Maurice Wilson

Penguin Books
in association with The Hogarth Press

Penguin Books Ltd, Harmondsworth, Middlesex,
England
Penguin Books Australia Ltd, Ringwood,
Victoria, Australia

First published by The Hogarth Press 1961
Published in Penguin Books 1965
Reprinted 1968, 1971, 1973
Copyright © Laurens van der Post, 1961

Made and printed in Great Britain by
Cox & Wyman Ltd, London, Reading and
Fakenham
Set in Monotype Times

TO 'C-G' JUNG

For many reasons, but here in particular because of his great love of Africa and reverence for the life of its aboriginal children

Contents

ACKNOWLEDGEMENTS

Acknowledgement is due to the following for permission to quote from certain poems: Faber and Faber for the extract from '*The Hollow Men*' by T. S. Eliot in his *Collected Poems 1909–1935*; Laurence Pollinger Ltd and the Estate of the late Mrs Frieda Lawrence for the extract from '*Etruscan Cypresses*' in *The Collected Poems of D. H. Lawrence* published by Heinemann

Introduction

This book is a continuation of the story begun in *The Lost World of the Kalahari*, but it can be read as a self-contained tale. *The Lost World of the Kalahari* was the story of a journey in a great wasteland and a search for some pure remnant of the unique and almost vanished First People of my native land, the Bushmen of Africa. In it I gave a brief account of the tragic extermination of this little hunter and rock-painter by the black and the white invaders of his ancient country. It told, too, how we found one great branch of his race, the river Bushman, extinct save for a few tragic units, and how after a search in the Kalahari we made contact in the Central Desert with a small Bushman clan. The book closed with an account of our short stay with these Bushmen, of their life, their arts and crafts, music, dancing, story telling, and of the film we made among them. It ends with our farewell to them at a place we called the Sip Wells.

The Heart of the Hunter begins where the first book left off. We are on our way out of the Central Desert. We are still the same company: Jeremiah Muwénda, our Barotse cook; John Raoutha-gall, a man of the Bamangkwetsi, his assistant; Cheruyiot, a Knipsigis bearer from East Africa, his employer Windham Vyan, an old friend who had come overland by truck all the way to help feed us with his expert gun; Charles Leonard, our South African mechanic and sound recorder; Duncan Abraham, a Scot, our indefatigable camera man; Dabé, a tame Bushman* raised by an Afrikaans family in the desert, who was our interpreter; and Ben Hatherall, also an old friend and my guide on many an expedition into the desert.

When this journey out of the desert ended and the company dispersed, however, I discovered that in a sense the journey had barely begun. I found myself compelled to go another journey, into my own mind and the mind of the vanished Bushman. At

* Bushman partly brought up by Europeans.

once I was faced as a writer with a dilemma: should I not divide the physical from the mental journey and make two separate stories of it? I rejected such a division in the end, because that was not at all what happened to me. Had it been knowledge, research, or the study of a scholar that I wanted to convey, I would not have hesitated. But I am not qualified for any of these roles. All I can claim is to have had a perhaps unique experience and the right to try and communicate, not knowledge, but the experience itself. I have learned, I hope, by now the danger and futility of trying to improve on one's own truth.

So the shape of this book is not imposed on the story from without, but is determined solely by the way the experience came to me. The way it came to me was continuous. That for me was one of the most significant things about the journey, and I felt obliged to respect it. Even then my difficulties were not ended. When I came to my experience of the Bushman mind and spirit, I found myself in the compromising situation of not only having to tell the story but also to interpret it as I went along. The Bushman used images and idioms which would be incomprehensible to the civilized man without interpretation. I cannot claim that I have done this well or with complete accuracy. I had no guide in this endeavour, for I do not believe anyone has ever before attempted it. But I had a feeling that I was possibly the only person who could start this kind of interpretation; who could be this kind of improvised little rope bridge over the deep abyss between the modern man and the first person of Africa, until the real engineers with proper suspension bridges should come along.

Through my childhood in Africa, through my mother's family who have been there since the European beginning, I had a link with the past, with the Bushman and his world, which perhaps no one else possesses today. For instance, I had from my grandfather a first-hand account of a battle in which he fought in the Orange Free State as a boy in 1848. Then my grandmother, her sister, little brother, and Cape Coloured nurse were the only survivors of a massacre of one of the earliest treks led out of the Cape of Good Hope by my great-grandfather in 1835. In this and many other ways I have only to stretch out my hand, as it were, to touch a day 120 or more years old. Other members of my family reached back even further, since I was the thirteenth of fifteen children. My older brothers in particular knew more than I did. They, had they possessed the will, could have done the task better, but unfortunately they are all dead; and I felt that unless I did it soon, it might never be done and something rare would be lost for good.

I drew deeply therefore on this climate of the remote past in my own life, but I had to draw also on my experience of other primitive peoples in Africa to get my bridge across. Where necessary I have not hesitated to use their stories and legends to make the Bushman spirit clearer to us. Yet I did what I did for my own sake. I find the thought of what black and white did to the Bushman almost more than I can endure. I could not, alas, bring him alive again: yet it seemed to me some atonement would be accomplished if I helped to see that the meaning his life held for him should not perish as he perished. I felt it as a debt of honour long overdue to gather into our own what was living in his spirit. And there is so much more of it than I knew or even suspected. One fact alone which seemed to me of an inspired significance was that, no matter how grim the fate or circumstances, no matter how meagre the scrap of living allowed to him, life was always worth it and worth fighting for to the end. Such natural aristocracy of spirit alone, I would have thought, should command attention in an age which, despite its advantages and comforts, has seen such a lowering in the human being's sense of the value of life that he is increasingly inclined to take his own. D. H. Lawrence in one of his poems said:

> In the dust, where we have buried
> The silent races and their abominations,
> We have buried so much of the delicate magic of life.

If I have rescued from the rubble of our past some of this magic with which the Bushman's spirit seems to me to have been charged or, as he himself may have put it, if I have 'helped the moon on her way', I shall be more than content.

Finally I have not hesitated to draw on what Stow, Bleek, Bleek's sister-in-law, Lucy Lloyd, and his daughter, Dorothea, recorded of the Bushman of the Cape and Orange Free State. Some day, when our values in South Africa are truly centred again, we shall put up a monument of gratitude to those four for preserving so faithfully and lovingly against the whole trend of the imagination of their time, the few scraps left of Bushman art and culture. I have indeed used Bleek's and Lucy Lloyd's *Bushman*

Folklore (Longmans) and Dorothea Bleek's *Mantis and His Friends* (Maskew Miller, S.A., Ltd) as the authorized version of what is a sort of stone-age Bible to me. I have only used the stories I myself collected in so far as they add to the light and substance of the theme I found there, and, I hasten to say, nothing I learnt in the Kalahari contradicted it.

For instance, Bleek never seems to have recorded a single Bushman story of how man obtained fire on earth. It is such a vital point of departure in the evolution of all cultures that its absence is almost inexplicable except on the grounds that Bleek's speciality after all was not mythology but philology. What is surprising indeed was that, being such a dedicated philologist, his mind was so open to other claims on his scholarship. In such instances as he failed me, I have not hesitated to draw on stories I have collected myself: I tell therefore, I believe for the first time, a Bushman version of how fire was brought to man. One day, after more experience of the Bushman and his stories in the Kalahari, I hope to publish a complete account of his stories. Meanwhile the stories I have recorded in sound in the Bushman's own words are safe in my library.

Then in describing this experience, the thought that it might help to preserve such few Bushmen as there still are in the desert, was always close to me. I am convinced that for him there can be no safety unless we take him first into our hearts and imaginations. The television film I made for the B.B.C. helped to that end. Already a few elementary steps have been taken by the British Government to protect him more carefully. But this work has hardly begun. The hope that my book might not merely start a skirmish but incite a campaign sustained me more than I can say. It is ironical that the 'Apartheid' Government, so much under fire for racial discrimination in the Union of South Africa, has done far more to protect the Bushman in their part of the Kalahari in South West Africa than the British Government has done in its own.

I have to thank more people than I can possibly mention by name, black, coloured and white, for the help they gave me on my journey. I must mention, however, my old friends Chalmers Robertson of Johannesburg and the provincial commissioner at Lobatsi, Arnot Germond, for major contributions to the success of the journey. I must mention too my friends 'Benghazi' Lloyd

Williams, Angus Collie, and the staff and pilots of the air services of the recruiting organization of the Rand Chamber of Mines for coming to my rescue in various moments of crisis on the fringes of the desert and flying me, my films, and ailing personnel, in and out repeatedly with such good grace and dispatch. Finally I owe an immense debt to C. Day Lewis for editing my work with such care and concern for the meaning it tries to convey.

Part One: World Lost

Even here in the desert have I seen God and lived after my vision.

HAGAR, Genesis *16:12*

1 Unexpected Encounter

On the way out from the central desert we had an unexpected encounter which, brief as it was, had important consequences for me. It happened on the eighth day after leaving the Sip Wells.

We were still deep in the Kalahari, moving slowly through a difficult tract of country into which the rains as yet had been unable to break. Since it was already late in the year, the plight of the desert was frightening. Almost all the grass was gone and only the broken-off stubble of another season left here and there, so thin, bleached, and translucent that its shadow was little more than a darker form of the sunlight. The trees, most of them leafless, stood exposed against the penetrating light like bone in an X-ray plate. The little leaf there was looked burnt out and ready to crumble to ash on touch. Under such poor cover the deep sand was more conspicuous than ever, saffron at dawn and dusk, and sulphur in between. There was no shade anywhere solid enough to cool its burning surface. What there was, seemed scribbled on it by the pointed thorns like script on some Dead Sea scroll.

There was no game. Yet the animals had been that way and clearly found it wanting. They had dug all over the surface with hoof and claw for the roots and tubers on which their lives depend until the rains came, leaving large holes and trenches behind. Vast areas looked as if a bitter battle had been fought over them, and there was always a moment at the climax of the day when the sun-stroke racking the earth produced the hallucination that one was moving across the pockmarked surface of some yellow wasteland of the moon. Even the birds were rare and inconspicuous, except for a vulture always dangling over the death-bed scene like a spider suspended from the blue on a silky thread of air. The few birds we saw no longer sang, and darted about their business with a desperate look.

What we did see in plenty, though, were snakes. In all the years I have known the Kalahari I have never seen so many nor any as

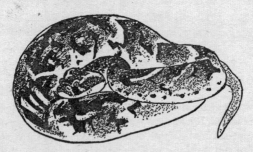

Puff-adder

splendid. I expect it was because there was little grass or leaf to hide them. The hotter and more barren the desert became, the more we saw of them. How right they looked in that desolate setting! There were horned little vipers as still as petrified wood and bright as stained glass against a setting sun. There were heavy puff-adders coiled like slave bangles made of a metal with a

Mamba

sullen glow, and large golden cobras pulling stitches of glistening twist through their torn cover of sand. Above all there were black mambas, alert, shining, and unafraid sitting upright in the sun. There was one even who clearly had been bird-nesting in vain and swung nonchalantly by the tail over our heads from the branch of a tree. Finally another with a glittering hieroglyphic eye shot underneath my Land-Rover when I drove between him and his hole. So fast did he move that as I saw his tail disappear on my left, his head appeared in the window on my right. I stopped at once, but already he had gone.

The farther we went in this way, the more we ourselves became affected by the desperation of the land. Though we carried enough food and water for our needs, the thirst, hunger, and fear of the earth became our own. What made things worse was that the formidable thunder clouds which came storming over the horizon in the early afternoons seemed powerless to break through the iron ring of drought around us. We would watch them grow until they stood over us like atomic explosions in the South Pacific. Their shadows would tumble from a far silver crest in folds of purple over our smarting senses, the darkened distances glitter with the flashes of their lightning, the earth shake with thunder and the wide desert suddenly shrink small into a posture of submission at their feet. Nothing, we thought, could now prevent it raining. Once even we saw the rain drops tumbling out of the base of the greatest of all the piles of cloud. They came swarming down towards us like bees out of a startled hive, but before they could reach us the heat rising upwards from the earth evaporated them. Then as always the wind got up, spinning violently in the dervish dust before charging upwards to shatter the great formations of cloud. We would watch them decline, torn and forlorn in the red of an apocalyptic sunset, and creep with the despair of the earth at heart into our beds on the sand. Before sleeping I would often think that my countrymen, of whom so many perished trying to cross the desert, named it well when they called it simply 'The Great Thirstland'.

Then, on the morning of the eighth day after leaving the Sip Wells, the sun rose faster and angrier than usual. There seemed to be no period of transition even, short as it is in these latitudes at that time of year. At one minute it was dark and cool, the next blindingly light and hot. One of the remarkable features of life spent in these circumstances is that nature becomes an affair of personalities. Any scientific notions one might have held about it vanish quickly, until there is nothing of the abstract left in one's mind. Sun, moon, stars, wind, lightning, and rain all become great magnetic beings and one's relationship with them intensely personal. For instance, on this particular morning, dismayed by the onslaught of the day, I remember thinking of the sun as a powerful being driven mad by excess, leaping into the sky, beating his chest and shrieking: 'Look! Look! Look! Here I am.'

As the day went on, the feeling of being locked up in a mad moment of the seasons increased. Within an hour it was so hot that the air began to run like melting glass. Long before noon the waves of heat were moving over the face of the desert so violently that everything upon it was blurred and broken-up until the whole quicksilver scene looked as unsubstantial as a reflection of itself shattered in the surface of a gleaming pool by the impact of a stone. The sky itself became a mirror filled with all sort of incomplete bits of the scene thrown up at it by the heat from below. I saw the summit of a dune upside down in the sky stand upon the top of the real one whose base had been obliterated by the waves of heat. Fragments of trees, shrubs, and dry watercourses, which had suddenly lost their grip on the earth, were seen entangled with reflections of their partial selves in the polished sky. One reflection which held my attention for long because it appeared to have no connexion with any of the shapes below and looked like some kind of Van Gogh train airborne on a heavenly journey, turned out to be the image of a deep, narrow cleft, still well below the horizon when we first saw its reflection thrown on the air. Once the outline of a tree filled the sky. As we approached, it shrank until it was no more than a lone bush without shadow in a patch of scarlet sand. It was only by forcing ourselves from time to time to look through this dimension of distortion and counter-distortion to the tranquil blue beyond that we kept some faith in the universe being about its business as usual.

By noon we were all searching for somewhere to rest our vehicles and ourselves. When a flag of green with silver stars and stripes showed up, I was prepared for it to be another illusion of the day, but nevertheless steered for it. Slowly stars and strips diminished, the green increased, and finally there stood, like a miracle before unbelievers, a number of camel-thorn trees in leaf. They were giants of their kind, cunning and very old, and what added to the wonder of finding them there was the knowledge that they were growing in a part of the desert which was not typical camel-thorn country at all. Usually they grow in great numbers in their own favourite sands much farther away to the south, where they give vast areas of the desert an astonishingly park-like appearance. But here there was only this lone outpost, the survivor perhaps of a great colony when the desert was kinder to trees than it is today.

We stopped close by them. Someone jumped out of a vehicle and threw a handful of yellow dust in the air. The dust fell like lead without scattering and clearly there was no wind. Yet we turned our Land-Rovers in the direction from which the wind ought to come if there was ever to be any again, and drove them underneath the trees. We propped open their bonnets and un-screwed their radiator caps. Almost without having spoken to one another, we threw ourselves down in our first shade for days.

My companions were asleep at once, and how I envied them! I could do no more than rest my body. My eyes would not even stay shut: they kept on opening and searching the sky beyond those incredible leaves above me for cloud. There was none except one slight white feather drifting down the blue like the emblem of the retreat of the storm of the evening before. Rain seemed farther off than ever. I lay there in this fashion for about half an hour, the high Kalahari noon hissing like a serpent in my ear. Then suddenly an urgent whisper broke through to me: 'Moren! Master! Are you awake?'

It was Dabé, our old Bushman interpreter, who had grown very close to me. He had come as silently as only a Bushman can from the tree where characteristically he was resting alone. Not a single one of my companions, stretched out beside their vehicles and breathing heavily, was disturbed as he crept on his hands and knees to my side. There, close to me, his lined and finely wrinkled face was puckered and creased against the violent light. His eyes barely showed, but the little that did was bright and alert.

'People! Out there, coming this way!' Straightening himself on his knees and waving a hand to the east, he spoke without waiting for my answer.

I got up immediately and walked with him into the open away from our sleeping companions. We stood in the sun and together looked and listened silently. I heard no sound except that of the

day now roaring like a furnace in my ears. I watched a tall whirlwind stand up to spin and flicker like a column of Old Testament
fire, its flames staining a lot of sky. High in the blue beyond it a
vulture mounted a vortex of pure air and wheeled smartly, its dark
wing-tips lined with sun. But that was all. I had not expected anything else really. I could not believe that any people who were not
specially equipped as we were could possibly be in that part of the
desert just then. Yet I knew from experience it was never wise to
doubt Dabé's apprehensions.

'Are you sure there are people coming this way?' I asked him.
'Oh, yes! I feel them coming here!' Tapping with a finger on the
smooth yellow skin of his bare chest, he answered without hesitation, and added, 'Men and women in trouble coming this way.'
I thought that if indeed there were any people coming, they were
bound to be in bad trouble. Yet the cocksure way Dabé said it made
me ask, 'In trouble, how can you know?'
'Oh, yes. In trouble. I feel it here.' He tapped his chest more
emphatically and then, a light ironic smile on his lips, remarked:
'But surely even you must know that people here would not be
coming towards us unless they were in trouble?'
Oddly cheered that he should feel free to score off me thus, I
said, 'But I neither see nor hear any sign of them.'

'You will. Just wait and listen, Moren!' He turned his head sideways and put a hand to his ear. We stood like that for some minutes more; then suddenly he grunted and said: 'There they come! Surely you must hear them?'

I still did not hear anything except the day in my ears, but I suddenly saw the wings of a bird flicker in the distance and a dark little body alight on the top of the skeleton of a thorn tree. It stayed only a moment before taking off again and vanishing sideways behind a swell of heat. I thought the shape of a man briefly darkened the broken light underneath the tree like a figure walking in and out of a burning oven, but then it vanished behind some denser growths and I was no longer sure.

Dabé, however, had no doubts, exclaiming quickly, emotion deepening his voice: 'You see! There they come, some more wild Bushmen!'

With that he walked towards the skeleton of thorn, calling out a formal greeting in his own tongue. Soon I and the rest of our party, now thoroughly awake, watched him bring a procession of little people towards us. They were a heartrending sight. Five grown-up men walked in front in single file. At first little more showed above the shimmer than the apricot gleam of their shoulders, the dark blur of their heads and the slender hafts of spears above them. Slowly their shapes became more solid and complete. We saw their bows held in one hand in front of them like some direction-finder of their determined spirit; then their legs, moving not with their normal resilience but at the slow deliberate pace of men so exhausted that they appeared to be completing a nightmare ritual of their sleep. As they turned to avoid a clump of white-thorn we noticed their spears were stuck into quivers crammed with arrows on their backs.

Between the men and the rest of their band there was a gap. They were close to us before the head and shoulders of the first of six women and five children appeared out of the blaze in the east. The gap must have been greater because, when the first woman came into view, she had already broken into a pathetic attempt at running to catch up with the men. The others followed close on her heels with a strange stumbling lope, uttering the broken sounds of the hysteria of uncertainty between an old fear and a sudden new hope. All of them were desperately thin, their cheeks hollow, lips black and cracked, and the dark brown eyes above the high

25

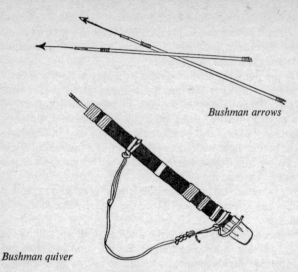

Bushman arrows

Bushman quiver

cheekbones sunk deep into the shadows under their foreheads. The skin on their bodies was rough, and despite the heat of the day and their evident exertion utterly without sweat. They looked as if they had been burned in a terrible fire and the light in their eyes was hardly of the world any more. I have seen it only in the eyes of those close to death. Yet such was their spirit that, as they stood before us at last on uncertain feet, they each raised a hand and politely gave us the traditional greeting of their race: 'Good day. We saw you from afar and we are dying of hunger.' I have known the greeting for many years, but only now did I seem to have a glimpse of the experience which had given it birth.

Their most immediate need, of course, was water. I was touched to notice that our three black servants had of their own accord already unloaded some jerry-cans of water and were standing by to hand mugfuls of it to the Bushmen as fast as they arrived. They drank it in quantities that would have killed, I believe, any other people in the same condition. There was not a grown-up person who drank less than a gallon and would not have drunk more had we not decided it was best for the moment to withhold it from them. The children, however, were firmly rationed by their parents and drank only half the quantity. Once their terrible thirst was quenched, they all sank down on to the sand in a kind of semicircle around us. The men sat with their heads bowed over arms clasped round their knees like long-distance runners recovering from the race of their lives. The women unslung the bundles tied in the shawls of duiker-skin on their backs and leaned on them as cushions. The children sat up tight against the thighs of their mothers, from time to time raising great oval eyes, shy with wonder, at us. The youngest woman of all took a small baby boy from her hip. His little body glowed like an apricot in the shade as she swung him to her breast. While he drank, the look on her face was so naked with tenderness that one felt an intruder watching her and looked away. It explained as no words could have done why the children were in better condition than the grown-ups.

They sat there thus, as if dazed with shock, not speaking for a while, though every now and then uttering wordless sounds to themselves. I was prepared for them to sit like that for hours, but they recovered with a speed which was impressive evidence of their quality. The first to do so was the woman who had come running after the men. She looked up suddenly to catch Jeremiah, our Barotse cook, who was filling a saucepan, spilling some drops of water on the sand. At once she was on her feet rebuking him in a low, clear but stern voice for his waste. When he went to refill a can at the tap of one of the main tanks in the back of the Land-Rover, she followed him, still protesting at his methods and clearly thinking he was unworthy of trust as a dispenser of water. The sight of the clear water coming out of the tap, however, was magic to her and silenced her for a brief moment. Then in a voice ringing with wonder she called on the others to come and confirm the working of the miracle. Those with us jumped up and hastened to collect around her, an expression on their faces which made us feel we had never known before what water meant in the first spirit of men.

Suddenly the woman turned away from the bright flow at the tap and began examining the group of Bushmen as if counting heads. Dismay showed on her face and a cry of self-reproach broke from her. Running to her bundle of skin, she quickly untied it, took five ostrich shells from it, rushed back to the tap and insisted on filling them with water immediately. That done, her hands shaking with haste, she plugged the openings in the shells with grass stoppers, ran back to her skin shawl, wrapped the shells carefully in it and slung it round her shoulder. At an astonishingly

27

firm pace she set out in the direction from which she had come, and soon vanished from sight.

We did not see her again until an hour and a half later, when she appeared leading a very old Bushman couple into our midst. They too were dreadfully thin; and yet, after having drunk only the water there was in five ostrich egg-shells, they had been strong enough to come after us. The old man was upright and very dignified. His behaviour was punctilious and formal, as if he bore all the responsibilities of a plenipotentiary of his race appearing for the first time on a special mission among a foreign people. His old lady, dark and wrinkled with age like a passion fruit about to fall, had the sweetest of expressions on her face. She smiled at each of us tentatively like a young girl at her first ball. Neither of them appeared fundamentally the worse for their experience. They needed no time even to catch their breath again after their long walk, but sat down at once to join with relish in eating the food we had distributed.

Meanwhile we had learnt something of their story. They came from a plain called after a fabulous kind of sweet potato dug up there three years ago. Their arms were not long enough to demonstrate the size of the potato to us. The plain was, as they put it in their tongue, 'far, far, far away' to the east. It was lovely how the 'far' came out of their mouths. At each 'far' a musician's instinct made the voices themselves more elongated with distance, the pitch higher with remoteness, until the last 'far' of the series vanished on a needle-point of sound into the silence beyond the reach of the human scale. They left this 'far, far, place' because the rains just would not come. Their water was gone; the *tsamma* – melons which meanwhile sustained them and the game on which they live – were soon eaten up. The roots and tubers we compared to potatoes and turnips were more and more difficult to find and in any case not enough for survival.

The game had moved away first. Only snakes, lizards, scorpions, spiders, and some ants were left. Then one night lightning flashed over the horizon in the west. They knew at once what to do. Since they own nothing permanently which they cannot carry, they could act at once. The men just took up their bows, poisoned arrows, and spears and left the plain behind them; the women bundled up in skin shawls their water-flasks of ostrich egg-shells and their stamping-blocks – the wooden pestles and mortars which

28

are their most precious possessions and badge of womanhood. Grubbing-sticks in hand, and for long hours with the youngest children on their hips, they followed their men. They made for the quarter in the west where the lightning flashed most. They had forgotten how many days they had walked towards the lightning,

Rock painting of women on the march, one apparently with grubbing-stick in hand

but they were 'many, many, many'. The awful part was that, though the lightning went on flashing along the horizon every night, they seemed to get no nearer the rain. Their condition steadily deteriorated, the country became increasingly desolate, yet they had endured this sort of thing so often before that they took it entirely for granted. They seemed to think it hardly worth the effort of remembering and certainly not that of talking about it.

Yet despite the lack of detail and Dabé's difficulty in coping with their dialect, we gathered that on this cloudless day without the least hint of rain their desperation was nearing its climax. They had just left the old father and mother behind, not expecting ever to see them again, when they heard the sound of our Land-Rovers. Yes! they knew about motor vehicles and avoided them because

Grubbing-stick

they connected them only with police patrols. No! they themselves had never seen any police, but some kinsmen of theirs had been taken away from their family once and had never come back because the police had caught them roasting a giraffe they had killed for food. But afraid as they were of police in particular and white men in general, they needed help so badly that they made straight for the place where they heard our vehicles.

We did not ask them what they would have done had they not met us, but the question provoked a lively discussion among my companions. The Bushmen had no food of any kind left. They had no water, and when I asked what they used instead of water they showed me some remains of a large root rather like an outsize turnip. They had six of these fragments in the slings carried by the women, and they were eighteen souls in all. By scraping the root with a wooden knife into their hands and squeezing the crushed material, they produced a bitter white juice which they said was better for thirst than water. Water, the old father suddenly interjected, licking his lips at the memory of his last gallon-full, was much too sweet.

For some of my companions all this was clear proof that the Bushmen would never have been able to reach the fringe of the area where the rains had broken. Others, led by Ben Hatherall, my old guide and friend, who was born in the desert and grew up with the Bushmen, stoutly maintained that except for the old couple they would have made it. Dabé thought so too. Judging by the speed with which they had recovered after their drink of water, before they had even eaten, the Bushmen were not yet damaged by their terrible experience in any fundamental way. The issue was far from academic to me, because on it might depend the extent to which we should still help this desperate little band of people. I was only too conscious of the fact that my companions had stood by me selflessly, for far longer than they had initially contracted, on an exacting and troublesome journey. Most of them were overdue and badly needed at home. Every night round the camp-fire we had discussed their need for returning quickly, now that our work at the Sip Wells was done. Nobody was more upset than I by the slow progress this rainless track of desert had imposed upon us. Both the heat and the loose texture of the deep sand crumbling in the sun slowed our speed down to half what it could have been normally.

If we now decided we had to help the Bushmen more, it would mean another delay. We could not do much out of our own supplies. After so long a time in the desert we had just enough to last us the way home. We would have to make camp there by the camel-thorn trees, turn back in our tracks to where we had last seen game, and shoot meat for the Bushmen. Should we not find game easily we might use so much fuel looking for it that we would be forced to make a detour to one of our emergency supply points in order to replenish tanks already emptying faster in the heat and sand than I had anticipated.

Such were my thoughts as I listened to the argument getting more vehement among my companions. I could not help noticing that those who thought the Bushmen were at their last gasp were the ones who all along had felt the least pressed to get home. Among them were Duncan Abraham, our cameraman, who longed to stay on filming in the desert, and Charles Leonard, the mechanic who was also our sound recorder, and who would like nothing better than to go on recording Bushmen music and folk-lore. Chief among the others was Ben. He made no secret of his feeling that, now our main task was done, the sooner he got home the better. Only the night before he had spoken with real anxiety about his land far away to the south on the Union border, saying that unless we made better time he would be too late to plough before the rains came. Had I not known them all so well, I might have suspected them of trimming their views to suit their individual desires.

Proof of how unworthy such a suspicion would have been came first from Ben. He had been stating his case with such ardour and conviction, only because he felt that somehow the honour of the Bushman was involved in the argument. He had immense faith in the Bushman's capacity to cope with the hazards of the desert. He believed as I did that the desert had proved the Bushman's best friend by being far kinder to him than civilization and its vaunted securities had ever been. To maintain now, as the others did, that the Bushmen would have succumbed if it had not been for their chance encounter with us, was to attack a fundamental article of Ben's charter of faith both in the Bushman and the desert which he himself loved above all other places. But once having spoken up for his belief, in that incisive yet always courteous way of his, he announced, almost as if speaking to himself, 'In any case it doesn't matter who is right or wrong. Certain as I am that these little chaps will be all right, I would hate to take a chance on it. We've got to get some more food for them.'

I was not surprised and yet was infinitely relieved. In view of what I owed my companions, particularly Ben, it had occurred to me at the height of the argument to divide my party into two. I thought I could send Ben on ahead with those whose need to get

31

home was greatest. I myself would stay behind with the others and two of our four Land-Rovers to try and help the Bushmen. I took Ben aside and suggested this to him, but he would not hear of it. If we made camp at once, unloaded two of the vehicles so that they rode light over the sand, and turned back to where we had seen game last, the delay, he insisted, need not be great. Travelling in the tracks we had just cut in the desert, we could make perhaps three times the speed we had done in heavily loaded vehicles over virgin sand. He would not be surprised if we caught up with some game early the following day, were back in camp by evening with enough meat to see the Bushmen safely through the rainless tract, and on our way again early the next morning. He was all against dividing our party. Later perhaps, when we were nearer home and in easier country, I might allow him to press on ahead in one of the lightest vehicles, but for the moment we ought to stay together; it was safer and would be quicker in the end that way.

I do not think we have ever made camp as fast or with so gay a spirit as we did then. Far from being upset by another delay, my companions, whatever their views on the argument just concluded, seemed to welcome it as some precious kind of windfall. It was as if a law without exceptions ordered these encounters with the Bushman in the Kalahari. Whether alone or in company, meeting him and giving him something no matter what or how little, even no more than a plug of tobacco, always made one feel fantastically happy. Long before I was ready to leave with the hunting party, Jeremiah and his two assistants, John and Cheruyiot, had built a kitchen and collected enough wood for a stay of several days. There was our large kettle singing away on the fire and the wonderful smell of bread cakes roasting on the coals beginning to appease the hungry desert air. Jeremiah was humming to himself, something he had not done for days, now a fragment of a hymn learnt years before from a wandering missionary in Barotseland, now a favourite tribal chant. It was difficult to recognize in him the person who only that morning had shown me the snapshot of his young son and said, as if it had all gone on just a little too long: 'Auck! He is a very, very clever boy! If God wills, I'll see him soon.'

Duncan Abraham, the feather of a giant bustard in his hat, was setting up his favourite camera and loading his magazines: Charles Leonard was connecting recording machine and microphones to the batteries in one of the vehicles. They had already got Dabé to explain to the Bushmen what they were trying to do. The Bushmen themselves, after food and water, were busy clearing patches of sand of thorn and scrub and building light lean-to shelters against the heavier bushes some distance away. They worked fast and neatly, while the women brushed the sand with their hands as diligently as any house-proud Dutch matron the carpet in her parlour. Dabé went backwards and forwards between the Bushmen and ourselves with an air of tremendous purpose and as if twice his height.

Duiker about to dive

The camp as a result was well found by the time we left. Ben and Wyndham Vyan, whose skill with his gun had kept us all fed for months, travelled ahead in one Land-Rover. I followed in another with Dabé and the strongest of the young men among our new Bushman acquaintances. The moment of madness had passed from the day by then, and the sun was still. In its long slanted light the smoke of our camp-fire stood high and blue in the golden air. Six other little columns of smoke surrounded it. Rising from the little shelters built by the Bushmen, they were more slender and sensitive than ours but as upright and blue. For me they made the picture complete.

As Ben had predicted, we came across game quite early the next day and set about getting meat for the Bushmen as quickly as we could. The first buck we saw was a duiker. It had bolted on the

Steenbuck

first alarm and was already running full out when Wyndham spotted it. Normally he might not have shot, because it made an exceptionally difficult target. Once on the run a duiker never stops to look back. I have seen only one exception to the rule in all my years in Africa. That was some years before in the Kalahari, and the duiker which had paused to glance back was promptly shot by Vyan before it could pass on the bad habit to others. Invariably it goes fast over bush and grass, its head down, showing little more than its back above the cover, all with a motion rather like that of a frightened porpoise diving in and out of the swell of the sea. It is this movement which made the old Afrikaner hunters call it duiker,* and which makes it so difficult to shoot. Today the shot was even more difficult than usual, for by the time Vyan had halted his vehicle and had his gun up, the back of the duiker was arching for the last time above a crest of the bush at the limit of our vision. Yet he brought it down with a deft instinctive shot, and the exclamation of wonder from the Bushman at my side was good to hear.

We went on for a while now without seeing more game or, what was far more discouraging, the spoor of any. When the noise of our vehicles finally woke a little steenbuck from his sleep and he rose out of the bed he makes more neatly and snugly perhaps than any

* Afrikaans for diver.

other quadruped in Africa, I felt I had to shoot. Yet I hated doing it. For me the steenbuck has always been one of the loveliest and most lovable of African buck. It and the Klipspringer are part of my own childhood world of magic, and this little steenbuck was a superb example of his kind. He stood at the end of a bare patch of crimson sand about twenty yards away, beside the purple shade of the bush behind which he had made his bed, and there he eagerly fed the precise little flame of his vivid self to the rising conflagration of another desert day. He stood as still and fine drawn as an Etruscan statuette of himself. His delicate ears were pointed in my direction, his great purple eyes wide open, utterly without fear and shining only with the wonder of seeing so strange a sight at this remote back door of life.

Remembering the gaunt faces of the famished Bushmen, I shot quickly before he should get alarmed or the sight of his gentle being weaken me. I would not have thought it possible I could miss at so short a distance. Yet I did. My shot merely made the little buck shake his delicate head vigorously to rid his ears of the tingle of the shock of the explosion from my heavy gun. Otherwise he showed no trace of alarm. I took much more careful aim and shot a second time. Again I missed. Still the little buck was unafraid. He just turned his head slightly to sniff at the wind raised by the bullet when it passed close by his ears. So near was he to me that I saw his black patent-leather little nose pucker with the effort. I shot until the magazine of my gun was empty and still he stood there unhurt, observing my Land-Rover keenly as if trying to discover what the extraordinary commotion was about. I believe he would have stood there indefinitely, taking in the strangeness of the occasion, had I not entreated Vyan to shoot from his vehicle much further away. Vyan succeeded merely in nicking slightly the saffron petal of one of the steenbuck's ears. Only then did the steenbuck whisk swiftly about, a look of reproach in his eyes. The sun flashing briefly on the tips of his black polished toes, he vanished with a nimble bound in the scrub.

I drove on very much aware that I had not lightened what promised just then to become the long task of getting enough food for the Bushmen and, now that the steenbuck was safely gone, more put out than I cared to admit by such poor marksmanship. Yet I was even more disconcerted to find both Dabé and the new Bushman apparently highly delighted at the outcome of the affair. Had they

35

been amused, I would not have been surprised. Indeed I expected my companions to pull my leg about the incident for days to come. Yet delight in someone so famished as our new companion so amazed me that I interrupted something he was saying, a wide smile on his fine-drawn face.

'What on earth has he said to please you so?' I asked the grinning Dabé.

'Oh! He is just saying what we all know to be so,' Dabé answered in the indulgent manner of someone instructing an ignorant child, which he and the other Bushmen at the Sip Wells had always adopted when discussing their own private world with me. 'The steenbuck is protected with great magic and very difficult to kill.'

'What sort of magic?' I asked, remembering my association of the buck with my childhood world of magic. 'His own magic or the magic of other people?'

'Oh. Just magic!' Dabé said in a superior voice, leaving unsatisfied the curiosity which always nagged me more than ever when the curtain between the mind of the Bushman and our own lifted only to flop back just as I thought I was to be allowed to see behind it. Yet my imagination had seized on the encounter more firmly than I knew. I know of few things more awesome than finding that all one's most determined efforts to injure another living creature have been unaccountably frustrated. Throughout the long hot day, at all sorts of odd moments, my mind returned to the vision of that gentle little buck standing untroubled amid blast after blast from my gun.

Luckily for the Bushmen, Ben and Vyan were better and more dedicated marksmen than I. Soon afterwards we ran into more game and within two hours they had killed another duiker, two springbuck rams, and a lone old male ostrich. All that meat turned into biltong should last the Bushmen well into the country where the rains had broken. Stopping only to disembowel the game, we turned back and travelling in the same tracks for the third time found them so firm that we made our camp at the fall of night.

2 The Heart of a Star

The sky in the west was red and the vivid light seethed round the peaks of thunder clouds massing once more all along the horizon for battle over the desert. In our absence the camp had been transformed. Apart from the kitchen fires, another large fire was lit in the centre, and by its light we saw our companions and the Bushmen waiting together like old friends for our return. Duncan and Charles came out to meet us with the news that they had spent a most productive day filming and recording. Both of them were amazed at the Bushmen's speed of recovery. Duncan claimed he had seen their emaciated bodies fill out all over with each bite of the food they had been given to eat. Certainly the voices which greeted us sounded louder; their step seemed livelier and their carriage far firmer than on the day before. They started at once unloading the game, and went straight on to skinning and cutting up the animals with skill and dispatch. I watched them, absorbed in the grace of their movements. They worked with extraordinary reverence for the carcasses at their feet. There was no waste to mock the dead or start a conscience over the kill. The meat was neatly sorted out for specific uses and placed in separate piles on the skin of each animal. All the time the women stood around and watched. They greeted the unloading of each arrival with an outburst of praise, the ostrich receiving the greatest of all, and kept up a wonderful murmur of thanksgiving which swelled at moments in their emotion to break on a firm phrase of a song of sheer deliverance. How cold, inhuman, and barbarous a civilized butcher's shop appeared in comparison!

The last red glow in the west died down behind the purple range of cloud, and it went utterly dark beyond our camp. Our own fires rose higher than ever, straining like a gothic spire towards the stars which were appearing in unusual numbers. Soon the stars were great and loud with light until the sky trembled like an electric bell, while every now and then from the horizon the lightning swept a long sort of lighthouse beam over us. At last the Bushmen stood up from their work with a deep sigh of satisfaction, scraped the blood from their arms with their knives and wiped their hands on stubbles of grass. The women and children came silently forward to help them carry away the meat piled on the skins. They vanished in the darkness beyond our fire, and only the sound of voices joined there in a common purpose revealed that they had not gone for good. Then the voices too faded out, and soon after the flames of their own fires began to go up one by one. As always their fires were more circumspect than our own. Ours was a cathedral of flame, theirs little more than slender candles burning in a night devout under stars.

The sight stirred me deeply. Even at the Sip Wells I had never spent a whole night in the midst of the Bushmen. We had pitched our camp well away from theirs for fear of damaging their lives or bending their natural pattern to our own special needs. On the whole we had kept ourselves deliberately to ourselves, and left it to the Bushmen to come to us rather than force ourselves on them. We had of course visited them too in their shelters, but always on pre-arranged occasions. The moment the purpose for which we had visited them was over, we had withdrawn to our own camp: once, when I happened on Jeremiah and his two assistants walking from one frail shelter to another with the air of the privileged slumming for fun, I had sent them back with a severe reprimand. The nights in particular had seemed too intimate a time for us, after so short an acquaintance, to intrude on them in their shelters. Accordingly my glimpses of how they lived through the hours of darkness had been brief, either at the end of a long day bringing the tired hunters and their meat back to their home or taking them there from a dance or round of singing and story-telling because a storm was about to break. Never before had I had them all around me for a whole night. Perhaps it was something unique and could never happen again? The thought was too much for me. I stood up from the bed I had been making away from the others to look for Dabé, intending to go at once with him to the Bushman shelters.

My companions, their nightly glasses of brandy and water in their hands, were gathered round the central fire. Vyan a little apart, as always before relaxing, was cleaning his gun and mine with the dedicated air more of an artist at the end of a long day's work than an exceptionally hardy and skilful hunter. Dabé was helping Cheruyiot to set up our field table. Ben was by force of experience and personality at the centre of the conversation. Against the fire his tall, broad, powerful shape stood out from the rest, dark and oddly magnified in flame. Beyond, the lightning was reaching farther out into the darkness: sometimes a flash greater than its predecessors made our own red flame pale. I walked over to them and heard them talking about the lightning.

'Is it really true,' Charles Leonard was asking Ben, 'that these little chaps follow the lightning about?'

As always, Ben paused before answering. So quick in his own reactions to danger and so swift with his gun, he was strangely slow in his approach to a definite expression of thought, as if he had found the process by long experience to be the most dangerous of all. But once committed to thought, he expressed himself clearly.

Yes, it was true, he told them now. Indeed they would be surprised if they only knew the immense role lightning played in the lives of all living things in the desert. It was in a sense *the* light of their lives. It was to them what a compass was to a sailor in a storm, or faith to us. In times like the present all living things in the desert waited with desperate anxiety for the lightning to come. When it did the transformation in them was unbelievable. It was as if suddenly they had rediscovered their lost purpose. No matter how

Wildebeest sparring

famished and thirsty, they would be renewed at their first glimpse of it. Wildebeest, hartebeest, eland, zebra, gemsbuck, and, hard on their heels, wild dogs, leopard, lion, and hyena would follow after it from one end of the vast wasteland to the other.

For instance, in one great drought, he had seen some thousands of springbuck nibbling, listless and gaunt, at the last stubble and scrub around an immense pan. That very evening the lightning flared along the horizon in the west. The next morning all the buck had vanished, but the writing of their spoor in the sand was plain: they were making fast for the west. In the same drought he was helping to take supplies to some 'Khalagadi, dwellers at one of the few permanent wells in the desert, where they were said to be dying of hunger. On the way he ran into a group of Bushmen no better off than those with us now. He gave them food and water and proposed giving them more the next day. That night the first lightning appeared in the west. In the morning they were gone, and their neat little footprints too were directed to the west.

'But suppose the lightning fails them?' Charles Leonard asked.

'I don't think it fails them in the end,' said Ben.

'But the end might be too late, as it clearly was for these little fellows. What if . . .'

'Look!' Ben began to bristle and to speak more emphatically. 'Look! We won't go into all that again. The end takes care in its own time of those that are truly of the desert. These little fellows would have been all right even if we had not come along for another month of Sundays. I tell you the rains are about to break. Use your eyes and look at that!'

His tone acquired a triumphant lilt as that of a prophet might have done on the appearance of a divine portent in the skies, for at that moment a prolonged and exceptionally brilliant discharge of lightning burst high over the horizon. For a moment the stark skeletons of the leafless trees seemed to stand with their twisted feet in a Wagnerian sea of flame.

The lightning vanished, leaving our own great fire looking small and Ben saying conclusively out of his reminiscent self that the promise of plenty of food and water on the spot would often not keep Bushmen back when the lightning called them from below the horizon after a long period of darkness and silence. It was like their God beckoning them: they could not help but obey. Even the tame Bushmen working close around the desert would be made unbearably restless by it, until one morning their white and black employers woke up and found them gone. It had happened to him with his Bushmen servants, and he wouldn't be surprised if in the morning we found our own Bushmen gone.

'Gone by the morning?' Duncan exclaimed, as if he had other hopes for them and himself. 'Gone without even saying thank you for what we have done for them?'

His dismay was so genuine that we all laughed. Besides, his last remark touched on an old controversy. Some of my companions were continually worried by the apparent inability of Africans in general and Bushmen in particular to say 'thank you' for any help or gifts made to them.

Ben answered him, not without a certain amused irony.

'But surely you would not expect thanks from anyone for the little we have done? Surely you do not want to be thanked merely for having behaved well? Do you expect a woman to say "thank you" every time you raise your hat to her? Well, however much we appear to have done for the Bushmen here, to them it is just good manners and no more than was to be expected of properly brought up people. If our positions were reversed, they would without hesitation do the same for us or anyone else, but they would not expect to be thanked for it. No! They would not risk insulting you by suggesting with a "thank you" that it was unusual for you to behave well!'

Ben appealed to me for support amid the laughter his explanation provoked. I have suffered all over Africa from the delusion of Europeans that, because the indigenous peoples of the dark continent have not the fulsome expressions for gratitude we have, they feel no gratitude. It was as unreal to me as another prejudice noticed long ago in Britain – that since the French had no single word for home, they did not really value their home-life. I had no hesitation in backing up Ben with an example of the Bushmen's regard for manners. I told my companions a story I once heard from Faanie Ritchie. She had known Lucy Lloyd and the Bleeks, who were the first people ever to make a serious study of the Bushman tongue. In order to do so they had gained permission from the government at the Cape to house at the bottom of their garden in a suburb of Table Bay a number of Bushman convicts from the national gaol. The Bushmen soon became very attached to the Bleek family, with the exception of one little man. He behaved so badly that the Bleeks one day asked the Bushmen why he was difficult when they were all good and helpful.

'Oh, but don't you know?' they exclaimed amazed. 'He was brought up by Europeans!'

'Did you realize that these Bushmen here know our Sip Wells friends?' Ben presently asked me.

'How do you know?' I said with surprise, for we were some

hundreds of miles from the Sip Wells, and the Bushmen with us came from even farther away. If what Ben's question implied were true, there must be a far greater degree of intimacy and communication between the Bushmen of the desert than anyone had ever imagined. More, it could be proof of the accuracy of the rumour I had heard that Bushmen from all over met at some great pan in the heart of the desert when the rains had been exceptionally good. My favourite hunter at the Sip Wells had spoken of it. Other old desert hands had mentioned it to me, and the vision they all evoked had haunted me for years. Before he had time to answer, I pressed him again: 'How do you know, Ben, and are you sure?'

'Oh! positive,' he replied without hesitation. 'Dabé has just been telling us about it.'

Dabé was standing discreetly on the far side of the fire but not missing a word of the conversation. He affirmed that it was indeed true. Not only the Bushman who had been on the hunting party with us but also the others had told him and questioned him at length about the Bushmen at the Sip Wells. Believing that our being proved friends of friends of theirs would give the Bushmen all the more confidence in us, I felt freer than ever to visit them in their shelters. So I told my companions not to wait for me but to start the evening meal. I got Dabé to accompany me and walked slowly towards the farthest of the Bushman fires.

Out there between our camp and their shelters the desert was as dark and still as I have ever known it. The only other living things capable of uttering a sound were snakes, and no serpent would have been so foolish as to hiss while about his business on a night so profound. There was no fitful air of summer even, no heat eddy of the frightful day spinning about to rustle what was left of leaf and grass on the scorched earth. But there was this intense electric murmur of the stars at one's ears.

Then suddenly, ahead in a band of absolute black with no fire or reflection of fire to pale it down, I thought I heard the sound of a human voice. I stopped at once and listened carefully. The sound came again more distant, like the voice of a woman crooning over a cradle. I stood with my back to the horizon bright with portents of lightning, waiting for my eyes to recover from the glare of our great camp-fire. Slowly, against the water-light of the stars lapping briskly among the breakers of thorn and hardwood around us, emerged the outline of a woman holding out a child in both her hands, high above her head, and singing something with her own face lifted to the sky. Her attitude and the reverence trembling in her voice, moved me so that the hair at the back of my neck stood on end.

'What's she doing?' I whispered to Dabé, who had halted without a sound, like my own star-shadow beside me.

'She's asking the stars up there,' he whispered, like a man requested in the temple of his people to explain to a stranger a most solemn moment of their ritual. 'She's asking the stars to take the little heart of her child and to give him something of the heart of a star in return.'

'But why the stars?' I asked.

'Because, Moren,' he said in a matter-of-fact tone, 'the stars there have heart in plenty and are great hunters. She is asking them to take from her little child his little heart and to give him the heart of a hunter.'

The explanation moved me to a silence which Dabé mistook. Afraid, I suspect, that like most of the people he knew in his life of exile I would scorn a Bushman's belief, he wanted reassurance immediately.

'But why don't you say something, Moren?' he asked, almost like an anxious child. 'Surely you must know that the stars are great hunters? Can't you hear them? Do listen to what they are crying! Come on! Moren! You are not so deaf that you cannot hear them.'

I have slept out under the stars in Africa for too many years not to know that they sound and resound in the sky. From the time I was born until I first went to school, I slept outside a house every night except when it was raining – and that was seldom. My first memories are of the incomparable starlight of the high veld of Southern Africa and the far sea-sound that goes with it.

I hastened to say, 'Yes, Dabé, of course I hear them!' But then I was forced to add, 'Only I do not know what they are saying. Do you know?'

Reassured, he stood for a moment head on one side, while the light of another flash from the horizon flew like a ghost moth by us. Then, with the note of indulgence he could not resist using on me when he felt his authority not in doubt, he said, 'They are very busy hunting tonight and all I hear are their hunting cries: "Tssik!" and "Tsá!"'

Had it not been for the darkness between us he would have seen, I am sure, the shock of amazement on my face. I had known those sounds all my life. Ever since I can remember we ourselves had used them out hunting with our dogs. 'Tssik!' repeated sharply thrice was the sound we used to alert our dogs when we were at the cover of bush, grass, cave, or donga in which we suspected our quarry to be hiding. Hearing it, the ears of our dogs would immediately prick up, their eyes shine with excitement and their noses sniff the air diligently for scent. Another 'Tssik' would send them to search the cover. 'Tsá' was the final imperative note which released them from all restraint and launched them after our chosen quarry when it was flushed.

I had always wondered about the origin of these sounds. Neither of them had ever seemed European to me. I had asked the oldest of the old people of all races and colours. I asked one of the greatest of all African hunters, too. They could only say that, like me, they had been born into a world in which they were already in long-established use. Stranger still, wherever I went in the world I found that, although hunters outside Africa did not know the sounds and therefore did not use them with their dogs, if I tried them out many of the dogs responded. They would start searching with all their senses: if I kept up the sounds for long, they became exceedingly restless, in the end letting out that involuntary and nostalgic whimper normally provoked in them only by the moon. That had deepened the mystery for me, but now I thought I knew: we had the sounds from the Bushman, and he and the dogs had them straight from the stars.

The revelation filled me with awe. I felt as if I had been allowed to witness the coming of the word in the darkness before time. I thought this was enough of magic in a day which in my encounter with the little steenbuck had begun with magic. My instinct was not to disturb the woman in so solemn an act of dedication. I thought of walking away into the desert; but the woman had already become aware of our presence. She lowered the child quickly, clasped it tightly to her bosom, and murmured in its ear some words burning with love, before placing it firmly in the classical Bushman position on her hip. Then she came deliberately towards us and, recognizing us, greeted us politely:

'I am only a poor woman and I have had no time to prepare my

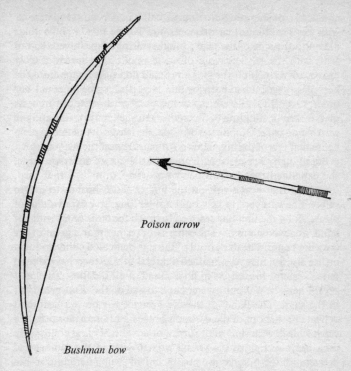

Poison arrow

Bushman bow

place properly. It is in an awful mess but will you not come and sit by my fire?'

She said 'my place' as though it were some stately country house, though it was just a patch of sand scrupulously cleared of grass and thorn and scooped out into a round shallow hollow. The skin on which she and her husband slept was already spread out in the bottom. Where their heads were to lie, branches of thick thorn were planted in the sand at an angle to keep from their faces the night air and the heavy dew that often falls so mysteriously in the desert. The man's bow and quiver full of poisoned arrows hung from one of the branches well out of the reach of young children; his spear was stuck in the sand beside them. The family's combined stock of ostrich egg-shells, fifteen in all, now full of water, were arranged firmly upright in the sand piled crescent-wise against the foot of the screen of branches. The woman's wooden mortar and pestle, or stamping-block as we call it in Africa, stood near by with her grubbing-stick or iron-wood beside it. On some coals drawn to the side of the neat little fire, strips of meat were laid to grill: with the subtle savour of wood smoke they spread a most provocative smell on the still air. Small and poorly appointed as her 'place' was, it had been arranged to satisfy some inner need or order. Over all this were the branches of a camel-thorn tree, its massive trunk standing between the frail shelter at its feet and the weather quarter. Despite the drought, the leaves of the tree were so dense that few of the busy stars got a sparkle past them.

Standing by her place with an endearing air of domestic pride, she explained that her husband was away with the other men, spreading the meat strips on the higher thorn bushes to dry in safety. She was certain he would not be long, so again would we please sit by the fire. She stooped to brush the clean sand with her hand, as a woman might smooth a satin cushion for a guest in her drawing-room. The dark head of the star-dedicated child wobbled on her hip, but his eyes remained tightly shut. However, we excused ourselves and moved on to do a round of all the fires. The last I saw of her, she was putting her child to bed on the skin spread out in the sand. The flame of the fire brought her bowed head and delicate profile out of the darkness of the night like a painting on a canvas black with time of the first mother with her first child. Only then did I recognize the young woman who in the moment of deliverance the first day we met them had swung her child to her breast, his body gleaming in the shade like a fruit ripening in the abundance of a well-watered tree.

At each of the fires we saw the same level of shelter, the minimum of material possessions and the women with their children, centred and at home beside their hearth. They received us with striking self-possession. They appeared never at a loss for a word, expressing themselves eloquently in soft voices and with many a vivid gesture. The consonantal 'clicks' of their language, which we either find impossible or manage to utter only with a grotesque effort, came off their tongue so easily that they sparkled like a kind of electricity between their quick lips. Despite their terrible privations they welcomed us as if they had riches and security for all. But as their men were still away working somewhere in the outer darkness, we passed on until we found by the last fire the old couple who had nearly had to be abandoned for ever.

It was impossible to tell from the appearance or behaviour of the two that something well-nigh fatal had happened to them only the morning before. The old lady was pounding some freshly grilled meat to pulp in her stamping-block, since neither her teeth nor her husband's were good enough to chew venison whole. Like an over-burdened housewife determined that nothing shall interrupt her routine, she barely greeted us; but not so her husband. He was lying on the sand on his side, his legs curled up and his body sup-ported on one elbow. Two little boys sat against him, each with an arm over his legs. The moment they saw us, they all sat up straight and he gave us an easy greeting. The expression on his face was wonderful. It was so resolved and free of tensions that I felt better for seeing him and full of respect. I asked who the two little boys were. He said, his voice warm with pride, that they were his grand-sons. 'Their place' was by the fire farthest from his own. They never failed, he added, his hand on the head of the elder, to come to him every night for 'some man's talk'.

The old lady ceased pounding at the sound of my question and waited, pestle suspended over mortar, for his answer: when it was given, she resumed her work so eagerly that the wooden block resounded like a drum starting up a march.

Dabé and I sat down near them. The children looked up at me out of their slanted eyes, examining my face without fear, as I told him I too would be grateful for 'some man's talk' with him.

For example, was it true that the stars were hunters? Did the little steenbuck really possess great magic, and if so, what sort of magic? Dabé, I think rather indignant that his word on the subject had not been enough for me, put the questions perfunctorily. A long silence met them. The old lady again stopped pounding. The old man gave me a steady look out of his wide eyes, oddly hypnotic in the firelight flicking on his face. My heart sank. I feared a repeti-tion of my experience with the Bushmen at the Sip Wells. There all my first questions had been met with a similar silence. I had to wait until we had proved over the days that we could be trusted before they would talk to me about the things of their spirit. I began to feel almost culpably naïve for assuming that such bold questions could draw an answer from a member of a race which for thousands of years has been so despised and hunted down by all other men. My only hope, I thought, was to remind him that we were friends of his friends at the Sip Wells and let the fact that they had freely spoken of these things plead for me.

'Tell him,' I asked Dabé, my voice sounding ineffectual in my own ears in the tense silence between us, 'tell him that his people at the Sip Wells told me about the first of all the Bushmen, Oeng-Oeng and his wives who would not put out the fire, about the little Oeng-Oengs and the elephants, the ostrich, and the finding of the first fire; Mantis and the resurrection of the dead Eland; the turtledove and the honey and many other things; but they never told me these things about which I have just asked him. Surely so old and wise a father as he knows the answers and can help me.'

At the mention of the Sip Wells, the magic name of Oeng-Oeng and this brief recapitulation of some of the great themes of the imagination of his race, the tension between us snapped. His eyes brightened, the old lady began to pound with vigour again, and said:

'Yes. Oh, yes! Yes! Yes! It is true: the stars are hunters.'

'All the stars?' I asked, my heart beating faster.

He paused for just a second, then it all came out at length. Yes! They were all hunters, great hunters, but some were greater than others. For instance there was that star there! He raised his thin old arm to point with a long finger at the brightest star in the Great

'*He pointed at Sirius . . .*'

Dipper. It just cleared the fringe of a camel-thorn tree and in the dry air was bright enough to lay a water-sheen on the topmost leaves. That star, he said, was a great hunter who hunted in far away dangerous places in the shape of a lion. Could I not see how fierce its eye shone and hear the distant murmur of its roar? And there was one even greater! He pointed at Sirius, the star of the

48

dog, at the head of the belted and nimble Orion. It was so full and overflowing with light that it was almost shapeless – a sort of careless gash in the night through which the brightness of the day beyond was leaking like clear water from a broken tap. As fast as the great drops of light fell, others swelled in their place to fall with a silky sort of swish on the bush around us. Yes! You only had to look at it once, the old father said, to see what a great hunter it was. Could I not see how fat it was, how heavily it sat there in the midst of plenty in the sky? He paused and I hastened to ask, afraid that silence might cool the subject: 'Is it the greatest of all the hunters up there?'

From the delight that shone in his eyes, I realized the pause had been a trap set to catch just that question. He shook his head vigorously. The greatest hunter was not there yet. It hunted in the darkest and most dangerous places of all, so far away that we could not see it yet. We could see it only in the early morning when it came nearer on its way home. There, there was a hunter for you! The old father made a lively whistling sound of wonder at the greatness of the hunter. Yes, just before the dawn one could see him striding over the horizon, his eye bold and shining, an arrow ready in his bow. When he appeared, the night whisked around to make way for him, the red dust spurting at its black heels. He broke off and shook his grey old head, as he once more uttered that sound of wonder, before asking as if the thought had just come to him: 'But can't you hear for yourself the cries of the hunt going on up there?'

I assured him I could. He gave a grunt of satisfaction and leaned back on both his elbows with a look on his face as if to say, 'Well, then! There is nothing more to be said about it.'

I took the hint and changed the subject. I reminded him of my question about the steenbuck and its magic. He sat up and beat the sand with the side of his hand for emphasis. Of course the steenbuck had magic, great magic! Surely everyone knew that; even the children, like his grandsons there, knew it.

'But, old father,' I insisted, 'I do not know it. What sort of magic is it? What does it do?'

He answered readily enough. But the subject now was far more complicated than that of the stars as hunters. The assumptions on which his explanations were based had no parallel in our own thinking. Dabé, who always had his difficulties with the dialect not quite his own, struggled valiantly to find equivalents in either Sechuana or Afrikaans for me, but I suspect often failed. For the first time I wished I had brought Ben too, because I had found in such encounters that, with his knowledge of the Bushman tongue and complete mastery of Sechuana, he could help Dabé fill the more important gaps in his interpretation. But I dared not interrupt the old father's flow while I went to fetch Ben, in case it stopped altogether. So I watched his eloquent face and gestures, listening more carefully than ever to his words, for Bushman is so onomatopoeic, so directly related to its meaning, that if taken in as a kind of music it makes some general sense even when the words individually do not. At the Sip Wells, for instance, I had listened to many a story and discovered that often the sound had conveyed the rough sense to me before Dabé interpreted the actual words.

Subject to these qualifications the old father's drift seemed plain enough to me. I gathered that the magic of the steenbuck was that of the innocent, the gentle and the beautiful combined in one. It was a creature – or a person, as he called it – too beautiful to be aware of imperfection, too innocent to know fear, too gentle to suspect violence. How it differed from the duiker! Had I not noticed that the heart of the duiker was full of suspicion and fear? At the first strange sound it assumed the worst and bounded away as fast as it could without a backward glance. The steenbuck, however, when disturbed would stand up and slip out quietly from its 'place which it made more prettily than any other animal in the veld and wherein it always feels itself to be lying so nicely'. It would stand quietly beside 'its place' and look without fear out of its great eyes, its 'little ears trembling and nicely pointed' to see what the wonderful noise could be about. The old father's eyes as he spoke seemed to become young and eager like the steenbuck's, his own pan-like ear to point and tremble with innocent curiosity. The steenbuck, he said, would stand there all the time 'looking so nicely and acting so prettily' that the person who had come hunting it would begin to feel 'he must look nicely at the steenbuck and act prettily too'. The person who stood watching would suddenly find there was 'a steenbuck person' behind him who 'feeling he was looking nicely at the little buck, wanted him to act nicely and prettily too'. When the person who had come to kill the steenbuck fitted the arrow to his bow and aimed to shoot, the steenbuck person behind him 'pulled at his arm and made him miss'. Yes, that was the magic of the steenbuck; it had a steenbuck person to protect it.

I should perhaps have left the matter there, but I could not resist an obvious question. Why if that were so, I asked, was the steenbuck ever killed? He looked at me almost in pity, as if I needed a reminder of the New Testament injunction that 'it may be true that evil comes but woe to him by whom it comes'. Yes, he agreed in the end, steenbuck were killed despite their magic, just as the duiker was killed in spite of its speed and suspiciousness. Yet more steenbuck survived than were killed. Certainly in all his long years its numbers had never become less. How could so small and defenceless an animal have survived in a world full of powerful enemies without great magic? His old eyes here were suddenly child-like with mischief and he looked past me, as if he saw 'a steenbuck person' standing beside me, to say he had been told I had tried hard that very morning to kill a little steenbuck and failed. Perhaps he had been misinformed, but if not . . .

That wonderful laugh of the Bushman broke from Dabé. The old lady, the children, the old man, and I myself joined in: we made such a noise that the people from the nearby fires and the men at work in the dark all came running over to find out what the fun was about. By the time the joke was explained and they too had had their laugh, which invariably caused everyone else to laugh all over again, the chance for more 'man's talk' with the old father had gone. I left them still giggling and went back to our camp.

Tired as I was after months of exceptional exertion without a single day of rest, my imagination was so stirred by the talk that I lay awake for hours and did not notice their passing. I had been in a similar state once before, at the Sip Wells. That was the night the first of the rains fell just at the end of the greatest of all Bushman dances – the fire dance. I had felt then that this search for the Bushman had retaught me in a measure the forgotten first language of things, and that listening to the rain falling I could hear the earth distinctly speaking to it like a woman after a cruel separation once more in her lover's arms. Only now, thanks to Dabé and the old father, I had acquired also the dialect of the stars and was listening in to their contribution to the general conversation. I thought of James Jeans telling me when I was a boy that every time a man lifted a finger he moved the stars. The important thing for me now was that the stars moved us as well and we all moved together. I felt a certain envy of the little apricot boy, and wished that I too had started life as god-child to a star.

3 Tame Bushman

As we stood drinking our coffee by the fire in the early sunlight the next morning, someone pointed to the Bushman shelters and remarked to Ben: 'Your lightning is not what it used to be. I see they're still all there.'

'Indeed!' Ben answered, not at all put out. 'They'll be there for some time now because there's no need any more for them to go to the lightning: the lightning is coming to them. Have you noticed the change in the weather?'

The first clouds were already sailing clear over the horizon. Now our attention was drawn to it, there was an atmosphere of excitement on the deep blue in the west, and the sun was up, not shrieking, but sulking in a surround of sulphur.

Ben's conviction that the rains were coming should have made everyone glad; but it depressed my companions for the moment, because it deprived them of their last chance of finding another justification for prolonging their stay with the Bushmen. Even so they managed to behave in such a way that the early start on which I was determined as a point of honour became impossible. First Ben and Vyan with their guns and some Bushmen disappeared into a desert which they knew to be without game; then Duncan and Charles played truant from packing up, to be caught in the act of filming and recording the women and children singing their lovely 'gemsbok song' with its waltz-like theme and curiously Viennese nostalgia. When Ben reappeared at last he insisted on observing at leisure our old-established ritual of naming our camps before departure and carving with an axe deep in a tree trunk the words, 'Bushman's Reprieve'. When we did get away the sullen sun was well up in the sky and the day already hot. The small huddle of Bushmen watching us go, their hands raised repeatedly in farewell and a look of profound absorption on their archaic faces, quickly vanished into the shimmer of another desert day.

All day long great clouds moved solemnly into the shining

vacancies behind us. They had a look upon them of battleships that had just successfully completed their trials. There was one, the flagship perhaps, which appeared to measure thirty thousand feet from its dark water-line to the admiral's pennant streaming from its foretop. Such power I had no doubt would break any blockade and bring relief to the Bushmen and desert in time. But where we were heading the prospect was as bleak as ever, and the great white day opened in front of us like the gates of a prison. The going was heavy and slow: yet time, for me, went quickly. Part of the reason was that I had Dabé beside me.

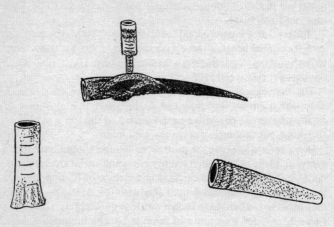

Bushman pipes

He sat at first sunk back into his seat, his greying head slightly bowed and those warm first-light eyes of his fixed on some point of their own within. The sight of him thus occupied with himself, rather than with one of the tasks we imposed on him, never failed to move me. Ever since Ben had discovered him at a pioneer homestead and brought him into our base camp at Gemsbok Pan, I had seen far more of him than any of the others. We had daily drawn closer together. Yet I had never been able to take his presence among us for granted. Seeing him when he got up at dawn or on my rounds of the camp at night, pausing to watch him where he slept in the incorrigible Bushman manner almost inside the fire, and so utterly at one with all the life that was and could ever be, I would experience again the shock I had the first time I set eyes on him. It was as if in him I met again someone I had long thought dead. Sometimes I even felt that I had known him before birth. That may have been because he was very like one of the little old Bushmen who had caught my imagination in the beginning, now so remote, on my grandfather's farm, or because he was the living image of the Bushmen evoked in my mind by the descriptions in history books and more particularly in the legends and memories handed down in my mother's family for three hundred years.

It was shameful how little I knew of the ordinary facts of Dabé's life. I was not even certain of his age. Bushmen have no calendars: they measure their ages roughly by reference to unusual events in their lives, as other primitive peoples do. Unfortunately the isolation of their desert world made it impossible to relate what was dramatic for them to events in our own. For instance, when an old rajah in West Java told me once that the first things he remembered were seeing the green jungle around his kampong white with ash and hearing his parents say the great fire mountain of Krakatau had woken up in rage again, I could judge his age fairly accurately, because the eruption of Krakatau was a world-shattering event. But when the old father we had just left behind told me he was still a little boy when his people dug up the giant root after which the plain he came from was named, the information was useless to me. All I knew was that some nameless calamity had forced Dabé's people when he was almost a man to throw themselves on the mercies of the few European families who had settled precariously round the permanent water-holes of a Kalahari oasis in the far west of the vast Bechuanaland Protectorate.

He had become thus, I guessed, about thirty-six years ago what both white and black, in an epithet charged with their unconscious contempt of his race's claim to humanity, label a 'tame Bushman'. Yet physically he was almost the perfect Bushman.

He was just over five feet tall. His shoulders were broad, hips narrow, his behind well defined, arched and firmly rounded. His ankles were slim like a racehorse's, his legs supple and his feet small with a high instep, and shapely. His head was round, well-proportioned, and covered with clusters of short black hair now going grey. His ears were close to his head, delicately made, and rather Pan-like. His forehead was broad, deeply lined; the face shaped like a heart. The cheek-bones were high, the eyes slanted Mongol-wise and lit with an early morning brown. His skin was a light yellow, finely creased all over. He walked as if his feet loved to leave the ground.

Only the irrepressible gaiety of the Bushman of old was missing in him. Knowing what contact with Europeans has done to aboriginal laughter in Africa, I had no right to be surprised. Indeed I have lived with primitive people so much that I have an inkling now of the almost paralytic effect our mere presence can have on their natural spirit. It is as if, when they first encounter us, the independence of our minds from instinct and our immense power in the physical world, which to them is not composed of inanimate matter but is another manifestation of master spirits, trap them into the belief that we are gods of a sort. Either they feel it impossible to be themselves in our presence, or they find it so exhausting to maintain even a part of their selves that they are compelled to rid themselves of us by cunning, force, or running away. The longer contact is maintained, the more subtly does this process work in their spirit, and the more devastating its effects. If only we were humble enough to realize that just by what we are we play the devil with the natural spirit of man, we could mitigate some of the consequences. But our unconscious arrogance is so great that the Bushman is left as a rule profoundly humiliated, without any shred of honour with himself, and often either deprived of the urge to live or filled with the lust to kill. Thanks to the fact that the European rule of conduct forced on Dabé was a relatively simple one, and itself operating in the natural environment of a vast desert, the process had not gone so far. It had just made him profoundly sad, and given him a look in the eye when he was not occupied that I could not bear to meet.

But once at the Sip Wells with his own people again he had slowly begun to change. The fact that we obviously were there not to dictate or teach, but to solicit and learn, had its effect. The pains we took to know about the ways of his people, the profound interest with which we listened hour after hour to their stories, our obvious delight in their dances and the immense trouble we took to record their music and singing and afterwards to play it back to them, restored to him some of the honour of his race. For some weeks, I truly believe, we put back the savour of his salt and made him feel what we all need to feel for our well-being – that we are important.

The change showed itself first in an increase of confidence. He began talking freely to me, who was with him most, without waiting on specific questions. He began to tease me a little, and then one day he laughed. Duncan was filming. As always while working, Duncan had a mind only for his camera: on this occasion, stepping back from it to survey the object of his lenses, he retreated straight into one of the most prehensile of all our many kinds of grasping thorn, 'the wait-a-little-bit' bush of the Boers or 'Ipi-Hamba, the where-are-you-going' thorn of the Matabele. Instantly his hat was whisked off his head, the straps of his light meter snatched out of his hand and his clothes held tight by the finely curved thorn. A look of outraged innocence possessed his features. It was all our Bantu servants could do not to laugh. They themselves laugh out loud over one another's predicaments; the more fearful the predicament the louder they laugh.

Europeans think this another proof of innate heartlessness. Little do they know that it is an expression of imaginative fellow-feeling inspired by the belief that, if they laugh over a person's injury, they help him to laugh at it too and so to get over the misfortune sooner. Also, the laughter helps to appease the forces that may have caused the misfortune and incite them to treat it merely as a joke too instead of a grave matter worthy of their continued attention. There is a less objective temptation as well. They cannot help being pleased in their secret heart over the indignities inflicted on us by the nature of Africa, and tend to regard them as a deserved corrective administered to us by their great mother earth for the liberties we continually take with her person and those of her children. They have learnt, however, that it is wiser on none of these accounts to laugh openly at our injured European selves. Although I am certain they had no fear of us, our Bantu companions now out of long habit constrained laughter to a smile quickly hidden behind their hands, before they rushed up to undo Duncan, who was almost zipped-up to the bush.

Not so Dabé, who had been sitting nearby on his haunches watching the camera with hypnotic fascination. Laughter flashed from him, sheer like lightning out of the dark – and he went head over heels backwards to lie wriggling with merriment in the sand. During the rest of the day, whenever he remembered the incident again, the laughter would bubble up afresh in him. It was wonderful to hear and to see, his whole face joining in, the skin breaking all over into innumerable little criss-cross creases and folds of the most endearing kind, and his body shaking with the spasms of sound breaking out of him. He laughed rather as the god who discovered laughter might have laughed his first laugh: it released a mood of light and lightness in all who heard it.

The next step was that he re-discovered what I had always understood from my aunt and grandfather to have been one of the Bushman's greatest accomplishments: a gift for mimicry.

One evening I heard our three Bantu companions by the campfire suddenly laughing at that almost girlish pitch their deep voices achieve only when they are inordinately amused. Dabé was facing them, his back to us. Against the firelight he was sharply outlined, gesticulating in a contrived manner like a puppet on a screen in a Javanese shadow show. Curious, I managed to slip out of camp unseen and to creep up among the bushes on the far side of the fire to where I could see Dabé plainly in the leaping light. He was giving them an imitation of Ben. Now Ben is twice Dabé's size and in every way an impressive personality. Yet I watched this little Bushman without stage accessories of any kind becoming the quintessence of the man, until he was almost a purer version than Ben himself. He was Ben eating, Ben getting up in the morning, Ben shooting, Ben delivering a measured and as always deserved reprimand to someone, Ben driving his Land-Rover in difficult country – so vividly that one almost saw the vehicle rocking before our eyes in the flickering firelight.

Then suddenly he was someone else. The sound of merriment instantly stopped. The shrewd Bantu eyes watched him closely for a while. Then there came a first tentative snicker from Jeremiah, and immediately a new gesture by Dabé confirmed the suspicion. Shrieks rose up from the audience of three, but I still could or would not believe my eyes. I appeared to be looking at myself shaving. Yet that should have been impossible. I always shaved at the very first light before the rest of the camp was awake. Dabé too should have been fast asleep then; but if what I saw was indeed true, he must have observed me shaving countless times. The blood rushed to my face and for the first time in years I blushed. I could no longer doubt. Dabé had become me. I felt almost as if my clothes had been stripped from me in public, the 'I' with which I shaved myself was there so naked before me.

It was, moreover, mimicry in depth, not merely a surface imitation of Ben's or my own physical movements. For instance, I have always found the minutes I spend shaving one of the most creative times of my day. Ideas bubble up in me, and the pattern the day is to take unfolds like a flower before me. This aspect of me was conspicuous in Dabé's shaving act: I saw myself becoming as crammed as a queen bee with cells of impending action, solemn as an owl with fresh thought. But perhaps the most astonishing thing was the absence of all caricatures from Dabé's performance. I do not believe that he was even tempted to comment. If he was, he certainly triumphed notably over the temptation. I had the impression that he had observed so acutely and participated so completely as to become what he observed, with no need to exaggerate or distort. Only thus could I explain why, after the initial shock of revelation, I had no sense of injured vanity, but crept unobserved back to my bed in the sand, enlightened and lighter at heart for the experience.

Nonetheless I woke up feeling some repayment was due to him. So I wrapped up a spare safety razor in paper and gave the parcel to Dabé, who was sitting by the fire with his audience of the night before. 'I believe you would like this for yourself and know how to use it,' I told him.

I do not know if his always lively intuition put him on guard, but he undid the paper as if an adder might be inside. When he saw the razor he looked stunned. His companions who were watching closely saw the point at once and roared with laughter. Then he too joined in, laughing without reserve at himself.

'Moren,' he exclaimed finally, shaking his forefinger at me. 'I would not have thought it of you! You are a very great skelm.'*

So gradually in these and other ways a natural pride in himself came alive again. Once it nearly had serious consequences. Jeremiah tended to have a noticeably superior manner with his companions, particularly Dabé. For long he never called Dabé by his name, referring to him simply as 'Massarwa'. This term is used by Africans to describe not only the Bushman but all the mixed peoples in the Kalahari living the Bushman way. No one suspected how much this hurt Dabé until one morning, after having been referred to repeatedly as Massarwa, he could bear it no longer.

'How would you like it if I called you not Jeremiah but Kaffir?' he asked sharply.

* A word for subtle rogue, used by all races now in South Africa, depending for its meaning on the tone in which it is spoken.

Kaffir* is the term used by Europeans to describe all black people in Africa irrespective of their race and origin, and has come to be used as a deadly insult among Africans themselves. Dabé could not have hit on a more accurate or provocative parallel.

'Massarwa!' Jeremiah exclaimed, putting down the saucepan in his hand, while John, his chief assistant, stopped working too and looked as injured as he did. 'Massarwa. You must not call me Kaffir.'

'But if you call me Massarwa, why should I not call you Kaffir?' Dabé insisted, the fiery Bushman temper of which my grandfather had so often spoken, for the first time visible.

'You must not call us that!' Jeremiah and John said together now, both their dark faces paler with emotion. They came belligerently to their feet and looked tall over Dabé's sturdy little figure.

Luckily I was near and stopped the argument before it became a fight by sending Dabé away on an errand, while I told the others they were never again to call him Massarwa and I would see that he never called them Kaffir. But to me, slight as the incident was, it was a shining example of a truth I have always believed – that one of the great hungers of the human spirit from the earliest to the most contemporary level is the hunger for honour. I am certain Dabé, Jeremiah, and John had been prepared to fight to the death because the matter appeared to concern their honour. I am certain, too, that no one will ever understand the complex and desperate situation in Africa unless he realizes first that at bottom it is an affair of honour. But besides the hunger for honour there are other great hungers as well: that for justice, for forgiveness, and the one that sums up all – the hunger for love. Some of those too showed themselves a little that day I left 'Bushman's Reprieve' with Dabé at my side.

When he had been silent for some time, I remarked cheerfully, since his old melancholy seemed to be joined to him again like his shadow, 'Well, Dabé. It looks as if the rain is really coming to your people back there. They ought to be all right now.'

'Yes. They ought to be all right now.' He answered without any great conviction, as if he and I inevitably must have different notions of what 'all right' was. He hesitated for a brief moment, his

* From the Arabic *Kafir* for 'Unbeliever'.

brown eyes going black with shadow from within; then he began speaking not so much to me as to that immense glittering overlordship of the day in front of us. His voice was flat, unemotional, and so without anger that I thought my stomach would turn.

Had I noticed, he asked, how everything in life had a place of its own? For instance, the springbok had their pans; the eland and the hartebeest their great plains; the jackal, the hyena, the lynx, the mongoose, and the leopard had each a hole of his own: the lion could come and go and eat and sleep where he liked. Even the locusts had their grass, the ants their mounds of earth – and had I ever seen a bird without a nest? The black man, the Herero, the Bastaards, had kraals and lands of their own, and the white man houses of stone. But could I tell him what and where was a Bushman's place? The echo of the New Testament cry about the birds having nests and the foxes holes but the Son of Man no place to lay his head, rang out so loudly in my head that I would have suspected Dabé of having heard it, had I not known otherwise.

Moreover, he went on, many of these animals were protected by the white man. If a Bushman killed a giraffe, an eland, a gemsbok, or even a bird like the giant bustard for food because he was dying of hunger, and the police discovered it, he was taken away to prison and often never seen again. Yet, if the Bushman killed his own desert animals for food, he was punished. No one punished the white man, the black man, and the Herero when they killed their animals, their cattle and sheep for food. But if the Bushman killed the cattle and sheep that came into the Kalahari to eat the grass of his animals, again he was hunted down and punished. How could such things be? Did I know that, when the first white men came to the Kalahari, they would have died if it had not been for the Bushman? The same was true for the black man. The Bushman showed them where the water was, took their cattle to grass and helped them to live. Once the Bushman walked the desert like a lion from end to end with no one to trouble him, but today every man and every lion was against the Bushman. He alone had nowhere to go, no one to protect him, and no animal of his own. Again, was that how it was meant to be?

Finally, Dabé went sombrely on, there was another thing: if the black man at his cattle outposts in the Kalahari wanted a Bushman servant he just went out to hunt for one and took him. If he wanted Bushman women, he just took them whether they had men of their own or not. If the men fought back, they were either killed or severely beaten up by the black man and his powerful friends. Should a Bushman kill his persecutors, the police were sent for to take him away. White men too would sometimes take their women, but above all they loved to steal their children. There in South West Africa, working in European households, were many many Bushmen who had been taken away as children and were never seen again by their parents. Even he sitting there beside me – he beat his chest with a clenched hand – was afraid of what would happen to him in this white man's land to which I was taking him. What would the white man do to him when suddenly they saw his old Bushman face alone among them?

This last was an old fear of his. We had had to have it out right in the beginning before I could reassure him that I would protect him and so persuade him to come. But it all went far beyond fear.

More upset than I dared show, I asked, 'Would you like me to take you back to your people we have just left and leave you there?'

'Moren!' he exclaimed as if he had not heard. I repeated my question and added, 'I am willing to stop and turn right round here and now.' I braked and the labouring vehicle stopped.

'Oh, Moren! You know I can't do that.' He shook his head and looked at me reproachfully as if I had been unexpectedly cruel.

I might have remembered Ben telling me that Dabé, like other 'tame Bushmen', had frequently tried to go back. Every now and then they found life unendurable in the rags-and-tatters civilization sprawled around the few permanent waters on the vast fringe of the Kalahari. When the lightning called and the rains broke, they would vanish for a walk-about all over the desert in the way of their fathers; but after a while they would reappear like beggars at their former master's back door. Never had Ben heard of a single one who failed to return, and that, of course, was the agony of it. They could not go back and they could not go on. Looking in Dabé's eyes, I saw a soul in hell; for hell is the spirit prevented from going on, it is time arrested in the nothingness between two states of being.

'Moren! Can't you do something?' he asked suddenly like a child.

'Of course, I will do all I can to help, Dabé. I have been thinking for a long time what I can do to help your people,' I replied. But I was compelled to add, 'Whatever I do, you must not expect too much. What would you like me to try to do?'

'You could speak to the government?' he answered simply, a flicker of hope behind the eyes.

'Do you know *what* the government is?' I asked, surprised to hear for the first time so big a word in impeccable Afrikaans and a rather portentous tone on his lips.

'Of course, I know perfectly well *who* the government is,' he corrected me deftly, indignant that I appeared to think him so ignorant. 'He is a very tall old gentleman with a long white beard who lives in a big house in Mafeking, and every year he takes his suitcase and goes to the other side of the great water to where his father who is very, very old is the government in another country. Will you speak to him?'

'I'll speak to him, and his father too,' I said, somewhere between laughing and crying: how could I possibly explain to Dabé the complexity of government? 'But don't expect much!'

'Just you speak to him,' Dabé answered; and with the certainty that I would, he recovered some of his former gaiety and interest in the world. I myself could not throw off the thought of what awaited him when the expedition was over and he must return to a life in which he was no longer accepted as an individual in his own right.

4 Ratel and Honey-Diviner

Dabé had come out of his dark mood just in time, for not far from where I had braked and offered to turn back with him we met the rest of our vehicles halted. My companions were sitting in the shade beside them and watching Ben talking to another little Bushman. He was young, about Dabé's build, and as gaunt and desperate as the ones at 'Bushman's Reprieve' the day we first encountered them.

'Poor little devil,' Ben explained. 'I nearly missed him. I was travelling at the end of the line and had just passed those thorn bushes back there when I thought I saw something move. I stopped to look and there was this little fellow running after me as hard as he could go. He was, as you see, without his bow and spear, and had only that Duiker skin there, which he waved like a peace offering in front of him, calling again and again: "Good day. I am dying of hunger." I think he was terrified of us, but his hunger drove him on. When he got to me he pushed the skin quickly into my hands and insisted on my keeping it, although it appears all the wealth that he owns. We've given him some water and bread and he's all right now, but the sooner Dabé can talk to him the better.'

Dabé bent down and they exchanged a few words in voices so low that I could not distinguish the words.

'He says,' Dabé said, standing up to give us the gist of it, 'that he left his wife and mother back there.'

We immediately filled a couple of jerry-cans with water, half a sack with our emergency rations of biltong, and followed the little Bushman into the desert. Behind us in the distance where we had come from, the thunder was growling now, but where we walked the sun set the sand on fire. The sweat ran from our skins; yet the yellow shoulders leading us remained dry. We were upon the mother and daughter before we saw them, sitting almost in the middle of a leafless bush to make the most of its miserly shade. The old lady was bending over sideways with a great effort to let her arm full length into a hole and was bringing up handfuls of cool sand with which she dusted herself all over, as a woman might with powder after a bath on a summer's day. The young wife sat beside her with her eyes on the ground, breathing fast like someone in a fever. Behind her lay her husband's spear, bow, and quiver full of arrows. Judging by the charcoal marks drawn on her forehead and

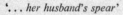

'... *her husband's spear*'

hollow cheeks, she had not been married long. While they drank and ate and filled their empty ostrich egg-shells, we questioned them at length. Impossible as it seemed, they were not part of a larger band: the man, who in our world would barely have left school, the young girl, and an old lady who could hardly walk, had taken on life alone in the central desert. It seemed to me as brave a venture as I had ever encountered, but neither they nor Dabé appeared to think it remarkable.

While they each smoked some of the cigarettes thrust on them in handfuls at the end of their meal, Dabé directed them carefully to 'Bushman's Reprieve'. With each puff of smoke, the savour of life seemed to quicken in their senses. I doubt if any human being has ever enjoyed smoking as the Bushman does. He smoked long before the Europeans came to Africa, and even had hashish sessions with his friends which he celebrated with the wildest of his dances under the moon. For these occasions, as the Bushman on my grandfather's farm had shown me, he built pipes of clay beautifully designed in the earth near water, lying down full length to smoke them to abandon himself between dances to strange ecstasies.

This little Bushman smoked our ordinary cigarettes indeed as if they were hashish of the purest kind. His first cigarette he drew in with one long pull, not ceasing until the fire reached his lips. All that time no smoke emerged from his mouth. I watched in amazement, thinking when he spat out the tiny butt that the smoke would follow. None came. The smoke had vanished somewhere deep inside him, and only when he spoke again some minutes later did it reappear in tiny curls of faded blue around his ears.

At the end of his third cigarette, he appeared to become quite intoxicated with tobacco. He suddenly stood up, stepped some few yards away from the thorn bush into the open, raised his hands above his head and turned his eyes inward so that the pupils vanished and only the whites showed under the half-closed lids. He began to sway rhythmically from the knees, and we saw the muscles in his stomach contract and gather into a round ball. This ball suddenly began to bound up and down, in and out, and from side to side of his stomach. I got the impression that his mind was no longer in his head and that he had re-discovered an older kind of consciousness in his solar plexus, which kept these inwardly turned eyes of his continually on the ball of muscle. For the movement of the ball was carefully controlled. In effect, his stomach was dancing a dance with a definite pattern. When he stopped, as abruptly as he had begun, his eyes opened as if they were emerging from a profound trance. He took a deep breath. For the first time I saw a sheen of sweat on his skin. Then he flopped down on the sand the beginning of a smile of contentment curving his crushed lips.

Dabé, wildly excited by what he had seen, leaped into the air and shouted approvingly: 'Oh, you Bushman! You child of a Bushman, you!'

'You may never have heard a Bushman say "thank you",' Ben remarked afterwards on the way back to the vehicles, 'but you have seen one saying it with his stomach today in the biggest way a Bushman can.'

But what was even more interesting to me was the cathartic effect of that abdominal dance on Dabé. It seemed to purge him of the last traces of the morning's bitter introspection. He began to observe the landscape intently again and to keep up a flow of lively comment on the scene. Thanks to the change in him, I saw something a few miles farther on which I did not realize existed in the Kalahari and would otherwise have missed. The Bushman's characteristic whispered whistle of amazement on his lips first drew my attention to it and made me stop the Land-Rover.

The fringe of thorn and stubble half-left in front of us was being violently agitated and then an animal burst out of it like a half-back breaking from the loose in pursuit of the ball. It had a shining coal-black face, pointed nose, and eyes like midnight sequins. Its shoulders were broad; its body long, with a skin so loose that it shook like a jelly and yet was thick and black as armour plating. Its back was covered with rusty hair, its legs short and shaped like a bow. The air of determination about it was extreme almost to the point of caricature. Seeing it streaking in the direction of the thunder I was so amazed that I jumped out of the Land-Rover to have a better look and make sure. The sound Dabé and I made tumbling out of the vehicle caused the animal to stop some fifty yards away and turn round. It glared at us utterly without fear, as if daring us to come near; but since we stood still it merely warned us with a sound between a whistle and a hiss to mind our own business. Then it whisked about and trundled on, the dust spurting at its claws. Even so I was not certain. The animal I thought it was normally wore a neat coat of grey hair with white stripes over a formal black waistcoat and trousers, not the rusty-coloured sort of football jersey of the little busy-body hastening towards the rain. Yet I have seen lions in the Kalahari with flaming red hair, so why not he?

'But, Dabé!' I exclaimed feebly. 'That was a ratel!'*

'Yes, Moren. He was a ratel.' He was grinning at me and then we both laughed out loud. Yet normally I respect the ratel too much to laugh at it. I know of no creature in the world so without fear, so dedicated to its own way of life and with so much of the magic of the beginning clinging to its spirit. I was laughing today because, in that vast, desolate scene, the ratel looked so absurdly self-important. Dabé, I was to discover, was not laughing at it but with it, because of some remarkable associations of his own.

'Phew! Moren.' He whistled again and said with a curious envy: 'That one knows what is good for him. That one can take care of himself better than any other animal in the world.'

'But, Dabé, if he is so good at taking care of himself,' I replied, dropping into the personal idiom he always used when speaking of animals, 'surely he would have chosen a better place than this. What can he find to live on here?'

'Grubs and beetles like that eye-pisser there,' Dabé said, pointing at an insect with long Chippendale legs and a white edge round its flat back, while uttering its homely Bushman name. The beetle, which defends itself by squirting acid into the eyes of its enemies, had appeared close by Dabé's feet. When he moved a toe it lifted a leg, tilted sideways and ejected at him a squirt of liquid fiery in the sun. Considering the size of the insect, the force and length of the jet were prodigious; but Dabé did not allow this

* Honeybadger.

The ratel

achievement to interrupt him. He went on calmly: 'Beetles, centipedes, scorpions, ants, and snakes. Oh, he likes snakes, that one! There is no greater killer of snakes than he.'

The skin of the ratel was so thick, he explained, that the fangs of no snake, not even the mamba, could penetrate it. When the ratel saw a snake, he would immediately go after it and not stop until he had killed it. He would even follow snakes into their holes and fight it out there with all the odds against him. He gave me such a vivid picture of the ratel eating snakes that I saw it gobbling up tangles of serpents like spaghetti. The ratel did not know what it was to surrender or to give up, Dabé told me. All the animals knew that, and small as he was, they preferred to leave him alone. Dabé had heard that in the days of the early people a hungry lion once attacked a ratel, and the ratel fought back so effectively that, although he was killed in the end, the lion was left too mangled to eat it. Since then even the lion let him be. But he had one great friend. Dabé paused dramatically until I asked who the friend was, then answered me with a question. Did I know a little bird that came fluttering out of the bush to perch on a branch where one could both see and hear it clearly, crying, 'Quick! Quick! Quick! Honey! Quick!'

That bird was the ratel's great friend: they were so close, you might say they slept under the same skin. Dabé held his forefingers straight, side by side and tight against each other, to illustrate the closeness of the relationship. Now the ratel we had just seen was in such a hurry because he was on his way to join his friend. He knew that where the rain was falling, there his friend would come to keep a pair of bright eyes on the bees making honey out of the flowers which rose, as I had seen at the Sip Wells, overnight out of the desert. When the amber combs were full in the house of the bees the bird would come calling for the ratel. Whatever he was doing, the ratel would drop it and follow, holding his tail slightly arched just above his back and looking up only to keep an eye on his friend. Every fifty paces or so the bird would alight on a bush, look back to make sure his friend was following, and in case he was lost repeat his call. The ratel would answer in his own tongue with a soft whistling sound to reassure him: 'Look! Look! Look! Oh! Person with wings, Look! Here I come!' Dabé imitated the sound so well that I almost thought the ratel we had seen had doubled back and was near.

Of all the sounds in the world, Dabé said that was the best to hear: friend calling to friend. When the sounds ceased, one knew the ratel was taking out the honey; but if a man could get near, he would hear the excited little bird bubbling with small noises like water coming out of a fountain. For in all the world no living things loved honey as those two did. They would eat it up side by side like the friends they were, each one choosing what he liked best.

Of course, the little bird helped men sometimes in the same way, but only when he could not find the ratel. He preferred the ratel to men. I asked why. Dabé looked infinitely wise and a little sad, remarking, 'Auck! Moren! You know what men are these days: they always want too much.' It had not always been so. In the day of the people of the early race the bird had preferred men to the ratel; but the bird had learnt since that men more and more took the best and most for themselves and left the least and the worst. Not so the ratel: he gives his friend what he gives himself, and as a result they are closer than ever.

Men had come to realize that the honey-diviner, as I called it, preferred the ratel to them. So they would walk about in the bird's favourite places, imitating the call of the ratel. The bird would come eagerly to them and guide them to honey; but when he saw how he had been deceived, he would tell the ratel next time they met. For this reason such men had to be very careful to cover their faces from the bird and leave no spoor leading to their shelters: otherwise the ratel would follow them and when they were asleep in the night bite off their testicles.

'And, Moren!' Dabé added, 'that one when he bites does not let go until he's bitten through. You can beat him on the head, stick spears into him, but he does not let go until he has finished what he came to do. I have heard my father speak many times of men who were punished in this way by the ratel.'

I thanked Dabé for telling me and remarked what a truly wonderful animal the ratel must be.

The honey-diviner

'But, Moren!' Dabé protested, with the look of the benefactor who has preserved his greatest gift for the end. 'I have not told you the cleverest thing about him yet. Have you thought how he gets the honey away from the bees?'

Indeed, I had not, I realized, feeling very much the amateur beside the professional.

'Well then,' Dabé said gravely, 'you must know it cannot be easy. The ratel's body is all right inside that thick skin of his: but what about his face and eyes and fine nose and that tender spot underneath his tail? You must know what bees can do to such places. So when the ratel has spotted the entrance to the house of the bees, he is very careful to approach it backwards, with his tail tucked in tight between his legs. When he feels himself to be close,

70

he will flick up his tail quickly, jam his behind fast into the entrance and before the bees inside can even wonder why it is suddenly night, he will let off one terrible smell after the other straight into the house. Moren! You cannot know how bad that smell is until you have smelt it! The bees cannot stand it. They fall down, all those who are inside, like dead ones, and the others smelling it from afar keep well away. Then the ratel turns about and quickly takes out the honey for himself and his friend.'

I looked into Dabé's experienced old eyes; they were bright and innocent with the wonder of what he had just told me. He shook his head as a man does over things too great for words, smiled at me and I smiled back. But the more I thought of it afterwards, the more wonderful it became. No animal is more of the earth than the ratel. It is in a profound sense the earth made flesh. No bird is more of the air than the honey-diviner. It is like a sliver of sunlit sky made alive. The two of them represent great opposites of life: one a kind of Caliban, the other a sort of Ariel. For me it was right that in such a reconciliation of opposites, which their partnership created, their reward should be honey; for in the first language of things, honey is the supreme symbol of wisdom, since wisdom is the sweetness of the strength that comes to the spirit dedicated to the union of warring elements of life. Dabé's story held the truth

71

Springbuck in the Pan

of a parable that has passed the test of time. The account of what happened to the men who deceived the ratel and his friend seemed to me an accurate description of what happens to the human spirit which uses one opposite to deny the other: like the men tracked down by the ratel, it is deprived of its power of increase.

The same evening we had another memorable sight. Because of the ratel I had dropped a long way behind my companions. Just as the low sun touched the great clouds following one another in line ahead from east to west far back where we had come from, we found ourselves on the ridge of an immense pan. Now these Kalahari pans are to me among the most beautiful sights in the world. No two of them are alike, and nobody really knows when and how they were made. They are part of the desert's mystery; and this evening the pan below us looked, I thought, more lovely and mysterious than any I had seen. It was round and deep. Its floor was level and smooth, a lovely chrome yellow under a blue and rose sky. Nothing grew there: it looked as if it had been scrubbed clean like some vast enamel basin set out to catch the rainwater which was expected to fall soon. Round the edges an outcrop of chalk below the ridge of sand glowed coral pink. The sand itself was scarlet between the charcoal of the leafless bush, and where the ridge met the sky it drew a ring of purple and gold twist tight against the blue. My companions were out of sight, but their tracks cut across the middle of the pure surface to vanish against the ridge on the far side.

Immediately below us stood a lone male ostrich in a frayed skirt of black crape, apparently deaf to the noise of our engine, with his head turned to the eastern end of the pan. I stopped the engine and we got out. We were hardly out when we realized why the ostrich stood as still as his own emblem on some heraldic crest. The sensitive air, already trembling from the shock of far-off thunder, was beginning to vibrate with a new sound. A strange drumming noise was approaching from behind the ridge as if a great army were beating a retreat there. While we watched and listened, the fine dust rose up swiftly to flicker like a sheet of flame over the ridge. Then a buck appeared, magnified on the skyline, the evening light burning in its hair. Others appeared to the left and the right of it until a quarter-mile of ridge was covered with graceful shapes and, as quickly, was uncovered again, for they paused only long enough to make sure the pan was empty before plunging down its sides. The moment their nimble feet found the polished floor, they danced with joy.

Behind them came vast cohorts of glittering springbuck. They poured over the ridge like a summer flood over a cliff, until the floor of the pan was covered with them, their delicate horned heads packed tight. When the last buck was safely down from the ridge, the mysterious urge which had set them running left them. Suddenly the whole of the great assembly halted and stood to attention as if drilled for it. There were now, I guessed, perhaps forty thousand buck below us. Dabé and I could not suppress a grin at

73

the experienced old ostrich, who looked in idiotic amazement at such excess of unexpected company. They stood there for perhaps fifteen minutes, moving very little, their fine heads held high and noses continually sniffing the air. Yet still as they were, the electricity of excitement in them crackled in the air over the pan. The old ostrich was so affected by it that he became restless on his bare feet, like a little boy who cannot keep still in church, and even Dabé fell under the spell of the charged singleness of mind given off by that immense assembly. He began lifting his own grey head and sniffing repeatedly at the air.

A last beam of sun came through the clouds, holding the buck like actors in the limelight of a great theatre. Once again their golden coats burst into flame; and then the first shadow of the night fell over them like ash. Suddenly the thunder far away spoke imperative in the silence and rolled from one ridge to the other. At that, one great ram near us broke from the rest with a jump high into the air. At the peak of his leap, he arched his back and shook out the ruff of snow-white lace which he keeps there for display when he sets out in spring to press his suit on the young gipsy ewes. He broke into that long effortless trot his kind use for long distance travel. He was quickly followed by others, the uniform gathering wheeling tumultuously into squadrons. They streamed by all round us without sparing us a glance, so close that we realized the evening light had given them an appearance of splendid well-being they did not possess, for they were all thin and hungry. Yet gaunt as they were, they were clearly undismayed: the sound of the thunder drew them towards the rain like filings of steel speeding into some magnetic field. When they were gone, they left behind an emptiness which was too much for the ostrich. He gathered his skirt about his lean loins and went after them with a long prophetic stride. Dabé and I were alone, to watch the twilight fill the vacant spaces until the pan was running over with evening like an antique bowl with mead.

That night for the first time in weeks we heard lions roaring again. At about two in the morning the sight of our camp-fire made a pride of lions deliver a solemn warning to us. I thought there were five of them and that they were travelling fast in the wake of the springbuck so as to make the most of the cool hours of the night. Their roar was so impressive that when I sat up in my blankets, well away from the camp, the distance between me and my companions sleeping by the fire seemed greater than when I made my bed the evening before. Such was the confidence of the lions in their power of command that they roared only once. The sound for me was a reminder that while the whole of life appeared to be drawn one way, we were heading the other.

5 Man and Desert

Two days later we came to a place called Tsane at one o'clock in the afternoon. Soon after leaving 'Bushman's Reprieve' it had become clear that we no longer had enough water and petrol left to take us straight out of the desert eastwards as I had intended. So we turned south to Tsane. I had arranged for some petrol to be dumped there for just such an emergency as this. It was an obvious point of supply: not only was it at the centre of the south-western Kalahari, but it stood at the crossing of the two main desert routes, one roughly running from east to west, the other south to north. It and the neighbouring pans of Lehututu and Hukhuntsi possessed wells that had never been known to fail and helped to support the largest concentration of Bakhalagadi, a people composed of all the pathetic remnants of races that had fled for safety into the Kalahari in the terrible time of South Africa's troubles during the eighteenth and nineteenth centuries. Tsane had once possessed a district commissioner, but had declined into a remote police outpost staffed by a 'Suto corporal and a section of indigenous policemen who from time to time patrolled the southern district on camels imported from the Sudan. The police, if the wind which turned the sails that drove the dynamo of their wireless set did not fail, had regular contact with their superiors in the world outside. If the worst came to the worst, one could use it to summon help by air. The great pan which gave Tsane its name had a floor so wide, level and firm that we believed the biggest aircraft could land on it. I myself had used it as a landing-ground many times, for as Ben reminded me, I seemed to make for Tsane only when in trouble of some kind. But on this occasion it looked as if Tsane was about to fail us.

At a distance it appeared as it had done the first time I saw it. Beyond a fringe of camel-thorn trees, where the deep red sand abruptly ended, the huts of the small police compound emerged from the heat smeared across the sky, their walls so white that they

Camel patrolman at Tsane

hurt the eyes. At the gate in a barbed-wire fence, the rows of round lime-washed stones on either side shone like polished skulls; and between the place and the diamond glitter of the great pan below it a row of trees miraculously in leaf stood with their shadows all contracted to protect their burning feet. No one moved in the compound: but by the well, queues of gaunt hump-backed cattle and goats and donkeys stood patiently head-down, first on one forefoot and then another, waiting for their turn at a wooden trough which some black men kept full of water drawn by hand, a bucket at a time, from a deep well. No sound came up from them, or if it did the air was too limp with heat to carry it.

Driving into the compound, we parked in the shade of another large tree at the back of the huts. The compound was immaculate – swept meticulously every day. Right where the barbed-wire fence ended, the desert took firmly over, scornful of so small an island of order. Hard by our vehicles some fuel drums lay in a neat line. Charles Leonard went over to inspect them hopefully. A look of disbelief appeared on his face and he exclaimed: 'But they're all empties!'

I quickly walked to the police office at the far end of the row of huts, tried the door, found it open, and entered. I was just in time to see the police corporal take some earphones off his head with an air of infinite resignation. He jumped to his feet, recognized me, and greeted me with a warm laugh. His office was cool and neat, he himself dressed in a clean starched uniform as if he were expecting a visit from his superiors at any moment, though I knew he dressed like that because of his own conception of himself. I have been to Tsane unannounced at all sorts of times and never failed to find him and his station thus. He insisted on giving me his best office chair and then explained he had no petrol for me or anybody else. More, the batteries of his wireless set were run down because the drought had locked out the wind from Tsane too. He had had no contact with the outside world for days. In fact his scheduled hour for talking to his superiors was just over. Not only had he been unable to speak to them: he had even failed to receive them, because of the storm of electricity raging on the desert air. We agreed therefore, that we would immediately re-charge the police batteries from our own and try to call up the nearest D.C. some hundred and eighty miles away that evening. But even if all went well it would take days before petrol could be brought to us.

I could not tell what had gone wrong with arrangements that had worked without a hitch until then. I knew only that it looked as if my companions, who had already had more than enough delay, were going to be delayed still longer. I felt it all the more because not a look or word of reproach came from any of them. Then, when my dismay was at its keenest, I thought of the two Indian traders in the vicinity. They each had a truck for bringing in their goods and carrying out their barter: perhaps they could lend us petrol enough to see us through? Happily, it turned out in the course of the afternoon that they could. The truck of one was away in Mafeking with all the petrol he possessed, but the other generously lent me the whole of his supply on the promise that I would replace it as soon as possible. Much as this little crisis mattered to me personally, it and our brief visit to Tsane would not deserve mentioning were it not for two things which emerged from them, both with a bearing on the central theme of my story.

The first was that Dabé suddenly and most mysteriously became ill. All morning he had been his bright alert self, but once in the police compound he changed quickly. There, surrounded by police and other strangers, he fell silent, shrinking into the background and swiftly diminishing in spirit and person – how alarmingly I did not realize in the midst of my fuel crisis until that evening.

The second thing was that, in order to solicit petrol from the two Indian traders, I had to go to the neighbouring pans of Lehututu and Hukhuntsi where they lived. While my companions bathed, rested, and re-charged the wireless batteries, I went first of all to Lehututu. I had done the journey many times before, and seldom without being made to wonder at the strange role of the desert in the mind of European man. Yet I had never been aware of it more keenly than when I was alone in my Land-Rover that afternoon. I know that, ever since I can remember, I have been attracted by deserts in a way I do not properly understand. I have always loved abovell a others what I call Cinderella country. I know of nothing more exciting to my imagination than discovering in the waste land, which the established world rejects as ugly and sterile, a beauty and promise of rare increase not held out any-where else in life. I am not the only one who has felt a strange desert compulsion, as the country round the three great pans of Tsane, Lehututu, and Hukhuntsi on this ample afternoon re-minded me. Many others, with an obsession even greater than my own, had been that way before me. It was the main penetration route not only of Europeans but also of Bantu. There, by the shimmering pans of Tsane, Lehututu, and Hukhuntsi, the mind of the invader experienced the first full impact of the desert, and, unlike the Bushman so at one with it all, was unable always to contain it.

For instance, there was a man who lived for many years at both Hukhuntsi and Lehututu. He was born in Britain, a professional sailor until he was cast up in southern Africa by the Anglo-Boer War. When the war was over he found himself drawn to the desert and impelled to penetrate it as far as Hukhuntsi, where he opened a small store and made a living as a trader; but his heart and mind were hardly ever in his business. That from the start was obviously a mere means to an end. But what end? As the years went by he cared less and less for this business. Indeed, the longer he stayed in the desert, the more he became engrossed in the sea. He did not go out of the desert at all for twelve years, and then only once – as far as Mafeking, whence he returned never to emerge again. It was as if the desert enabled him to be more of a sailor, in his own private conception of the role, than the sea itself had ever done. There, he never forgot a ship or the name of a person he had sailed with – not even the names of the officers and men of the British Army he had helped to ferry from England to the Cape in the war behind him.

Sometimes, I was told by the only European who succeeded in forming an acquaintanceship with him, he would walk for hours at night round and round the little square building with walls of dung and roof of iron that was home to him, muttering what sounded like a sort of incantation. It was a recital of the names of the ships and the men who had sailed in them with him. By constant repetition the recital had become something far more than an exercise of memory. With the night plover piping a strange kind of sea-summons in the desert all around him, it had the magic of a ritual designed to release a Merlin from his mound.

So deep became his absorption with the sea that all his energies were finally mobilized into defending it against the pull of the world without. I am assured he hardly ever looked a woman in the face and certainly never slept with one. He lived as alone inside himself as the sole survivor of a ship-wreck adrift on a raft in an empty ocean. He could hardly bear even to cook for himself any more. Yet when the news of the First World War reached him, he instantly recovered a purpose outside himself and was stimulated to invent on paper a series of Jules Verne devices to aid Britain in her war at sea. He wrote a great number of letters offering his inventions to the Admiralty. Their rejection confirmed his distaste and suspicion of the world outside. When the last war broke out, he was impelled to a final outburst of inventive activity. He believed he had invented the perfect anti-submarine weapon; and from that moment he lived in terror lest enemy agents should penetrate the desert and take his wonderful device from him. Every one of the rare Europeans who crossed the desert became suspect, and he was reputed to have scared some away by firing his rusty rifle when they were still at a great distance.

I myself once narrowly escaped being shot at, and was fortunate to receive no more than an unyielding refusal to come out of his locked room to speak to me. Soon afterwards this man gave up trading altogether; he went to live in a corrugated iron shelter next to his old store, which was taken over by an adventurous Indian trader from Bombay. Would I, I wondered on my way there, be shot at or be met in peace and be permitted to talk to him? The hospitable Indian told me the man was dead, and gave me such a description of his last years that I realized he was at sea to the end. I have thought of him ever since as a soul lost by drowning.

Then there was a man of a different sort. A member of a family with a long and distinguished record as missionaries of a Protestant society in Africa, he had once served in the desert as an officer of the administration. Gradually he turned his back on the world and the people from whom he had come, finding that he could make his peace with whatever the desert meant to him only by becoming a sort of European Bushman. He took to having Bushman wives: with the zeal of the convert, he became almost more of a Bushman than the Bushman himself. Indeed, as so often happens with the converted, he was apt to favour the negative rather than the positive aspects of his conversion. He lived, I am told, in frightening squalor. Communication between him and his own kind quickly broke down.

On the rare occasions he reappeared in a more civilized community on the eastern approaches to the desert, he looked dazed like someone who had just crawled out of a labyrinthine pot-hole into which he had fallen deep in the earth. He would walk from one sun-drenched little store to the other, doing his modest shopping, as if blinded by the light of day. One of my own friends, who had known him and his civilized accomplishments in the past, confessed to a sensation of awe on seeing him thus. He felt as if he were witnessing the return of a kind of twentieth-century Orpheus, who had not only failed to retrieve his Eurydice but lost his lute as well in an underworld where ordinary men would not dare to venture. Whatever one felt about his way of life, however much one abhorred it, my friend emphasized, one had to concede that it needed a certain courage to do that kind of thing in southern Africa. My friend would have liked to speak to the man and try to help, yet could never bring himself to do so. He was always forced to turn away, and afterwards was ashamed of the inhibitions which stifled so natural an impulse at birth.

I had longed to meet this man, because I was convinced he would be able to speak of the Bushman as no one else, not even they themselves, could have spoken. I regarded him as a pioneer with an experience too precious to be wasted. Perhaps over-naïvely, I had the feeling that if only he could talk about it to someone of his own kind who would value what he had to say, he might discover some objective meaning in the life he was leading. Such a discovery, to use the simile of my friend, could perhaps restore his lute to him, even if it could not give him back his Eurydice. But I failed to find him; and on this bright day in the surroundings once so familiar to him, thinking of his rejection of all that the European in southern Africa values most, I seemed to have an inkling of what made one of the most civilized of modern poets write:

> And now what will become of us without barbarians?
> Those people were some sort of a solution.

Another who came this way, though finally he settled in the Kalahari farther north, was a friend of mine, Tom Hardbattle. I have always suspected that there are names which cannot fail to have a profound influence on the character of the persons on whom they are bestowed. Tom's, I believe, was the kind of name on which a personality turns. I know nothing about his childhood, but I would not be surprised to learn that he was in battle from the start, for in all the years I have known him he has been hard at war of some kind. An ex-London policeman who fought with a City contingent in the South African War at the beginning of the century, he could not face returning to a metropolitan livelihood. He had had enough of houses, chimney pots, and a measured beat in a narrow street. He loved the openness of the South African scene and instinctively made for the widest and emptiest part of it. Hard by Gemsbok Pan, where we had our base for our final probe into the central desert, and where Cecil Rhodes in the nineties had established some seven Afrikaner families at the only permanent waters in the western Kalahari, as a buffer against German expansion from South West Africa, he started a cattle ranch. He had a terrible struggle to make a living. It took him forty-five years to attain security and some comfort of life, but he was never tempted to give up and return to England.

'I found all I wanted here, and here I'll stay until the end,' he told me in one of his last letters. But what had he wanted? It is easy to answer negatively – that it was clearly something the outside world in his view could not give him. But what? A personal challenge and call to individual battle? I am certain that had much to do with it. I suspect it was also the old story of the implacable necessity of a man having honour within his own natural spirit. A man cannot live and temper his metal without such honour. There is deep in him a sense of heroic quest; and our modern way of life, with its emphasis on security, its distrust of the unknown and its elevation of abstract collective values, has repressed the heroic impulse to a degree that may produce the most dangerous consequences. One has only to observe the great paradox of our time: how, in the midst of the imposing display of public welfare, the private sense of neglect and insecurity has grown in the heart of the individual man. I do believe that it was an awareness of some such danger to him which sent Tom to battle alone in the desert. But then, why the desert? Was not that in itself a kind of running away, a lack of heroism? Is it not more heroic today to walk as an individual in the collective way, and to arrive at the end of the common road a person not only intact but enlarged? The answer, perhaps, is best left until I have mustered all my examples and finished this sketch of a remarkable life.

As if battle with the physical desert were not enough, Tom was soon in battle of another kind. He began to live openly with Bushman women. Such public opinion as existed in that remote world, in the shape of the Calvinist outlook of his pioneer neighbours, was profoundly shocked. That sort of thing was bad enough done on the sly, but done openly was unforgivable. Tom refused to let public opinion create a sense of shame in him over something that appeared perfectly natural to him.

This question of shame was the heart of the matter. Had he allowed public opinion to convince him that he ought to be ashamed, he would – I believe – have vanished from the daylight of his kind as surely as that descendant of missionaries I have mentioned vanished from the light of his own day. People waited in vain for his nerve to be broken. He continued to enjoy his hard life, and to have success in a world where there was little: the exuberance of his spirits seemed to his neighbours the product of an almost treasonable collaboration on the part of Providence. Once in my presence, at a small gathering at Gemsbok Pan where almost everyone had had a brandy and water too many and the talk turned drearily to sex, one man asked Tom: 'Is it true that once you have slept with a Bushman woman, it spoils white women for you for ever?' 'I can't say,' Tom answered blandly, 'I've never slept with a white woman.'

Tom never disowned the children of these unions. He gave them a proper education and provided as well as he could for their future in the desert. Finally, he alone in that part of the world openly championed the Bushman and fought the rules and regulations which seemed to him unjust to them. Old and in ill-health,* he remained unbroken in spirit, a staunch ally in the battle for recognition of the Bushman's claim to a life of his own. When he said he had found all he wanted in the desert, I suspect it was because it enabled him to be a better kind of policeman than he could have been in the world outside, walking a unique beat there for sixty years and taking into his protection some of those cruelly uncared-for children of life around him.

One more example is needed to illustrate the extreme diversity of type drawn to the desert. There came this way, after the war at the beginning of the century, an Australian who was mentally and physically the toughest human being I have ever seen. He began his career in the southern part of the desert, digging wells for profit. On one of his well-digging excursions he would have died had it not been for an old Bushman lady, who found him nearly dead of thirst and dragged him to a Sip Well where she revived him with secret water sucked out of the sand through a pipe, and kept him there for a week until he was strong enough to go on.

In the course of time a formidable round of activity took him everywhere in the desert. He came to know it better than perhaps any other European has known it. He knew it so well in the end that he was supremely contemptuous of its hazards. Once he trekked across a waterless stretch of several hundreds of miles with only a tin of sardines and a tin of condensed milk in his pockets. He could afford such risks because of his remarkable knowledge of the plants that provide the Bushman and the animals with moisture and food in the long dry seasons. Much of this exceptional knowledge he owed to his passion for sleeping wherever he went with Bushman, Hottentot, 'Chuana, 'Khalagadi and Herero women. His first action on arriving at a water-point reliable enough for human beings to establish themselves near it, was to find a woman to live with him for the duration of his stay. I myself have yet to discover

* He died some months ago. When his final illness was upon him, he went out to Johannesburg to consult some of the greatest specialists in South Africa. But he had no faith in them and could not bear life in a city. Soon he was back in the desert and on the first day home covered his aching head and face with Bushman ointment. 'I have had my first good night since I left,' he said the next day. Not long after that, he died – with a smile.

such a water-point which is not associated with one or more of his singular exploits with the women of the Kalahari.

The desert can be all things to man; but above all it is a symbol of what has been most deeply denied in men's own spirit: it is a kind of bright mirror wherein they see the arid reflection of their own rejected and uncared-for selves. For this Australian the desert was sex. It was as if he felt that the sort of life he came from had made a desert of sex and called it morality, and only by an unconditional surrender to his impulses could he make the wilderness within himself flower again. Certainly one cannot have crossed his reckless tracks all over the desert, as I have often done, without getting some idea of the terrible power of his compulsion from the unscrupulous methods he used for getting his women, and the prodigiousness of his affairs. He left numerous half-caste children behind, without apparently ever giving them or their mothers any special thought or help. Some of those I have seen were disturbingly handsome, their eyes a strange unresolved compound of blue and black, and deep in them a kind of nostalgia for a kingdom of their own by the sea.

Frank Debenham, when we were in the Kalahari together, saw one of this Australian's daughters by a Hottentot woman at the very Hukhuntsi to which I was now heading. Debenham went there to visit what is reputed to be the last free community of Hottentots left in the world. There are barely five hundred of this unique and irreplaceable copper race, which once peopled a large part of southern Africa, assembled in the neighbourhood of the pan: even that small number is apparently too much for the greedy life of our time, since it is dwindling fast. Not only do they have few children and a high mortality rate, but also, when a young man ventures into the world outside, the community will not have him back again. Such a person, I was told, is more dead than their dead and no one will ever speak his name again. Only in this way, the community claims, can it preserve intact the spirit inherited from their great beggetter, Heitse-Eibib.

However, they must have made an exception of women and babies, for when they were gathered round him, Debenham found himself looking into a pair of the bluest of blue Australian eyes, slanted Mongol-wise in a fresh young girl's face with a smooth skin of a subtle tan, high cheek-bones, an Aryan nose, and the mouth and bearing of a princess. She was one of his compatriot's children, and, he assured me, one of the most beautiful girls he had ever seen. The encounter made a profound impression on him: for many days after, we talked about her and wondered over her future. I myself always regretted that on the day Debenham met her I was away on a probe into the desert far to the west. Though I visited Hukhuntsi repeatedly afterwards, she was never there. No one would admit any knowledge of her or her whereabouts. On this occasion, the young Indian trader who was a newcomer to the pan said, I believe truthfully, he too had never heard of her.

While his 'Chuana helpers syphoned out petrol for me, I drove to the Hottentot settlement, thinking I might have better luck and find her there. The crude huts were mostly silent, sealed with mats over the entrances. A few wrinkled and despondent old women looking after some solemn fat-bellied children were about, but they could or would tell me nothing. All the rest of the community were away hunting the game on which their lives depended and which had moved deeper into the desert because of the drought. There seemed no help for it. I was not meant to see her: she appeared to have vanished irrevocably into the blue of the southern desert. I regretted it all the more because I believe hers to have been the kind of beauty in which the future of a whole continent sings, exhorting its children to renounce what is out of accord with the grand design of life. But who can know for certain? All the generous young Indian could contribute on my return was to exclaim with a passion totally unexpected in a person with so gentle a manner: 'But why bother, sir? They are all terrible, terrible people, these Hottentots. They are, I assure you, sir, useless, useless people! They won't stay still to do honest work like other men. They spend their lives hunting and killing animals, and then eat and dance and sleep by the kill, their bellies stretched to bursting point.'

The division, of course, is deep and of eternal importance. Cain and Abel, Jacob and Esau, settler and Bushman, peasant and hunter, face one another in each of us, an abyss of deceit and murder in between. Who and what can bridge it? There was no answer ready in my heart, as I drove towards Tsane in the long level light of an evening that had utterly forgiven the day its heat. I knew only that the meaning of life for me is in the search for the answer, and that the search had brought me there.

I returned to Tsane, just as the 'Suto corporal was turning out a guard of two of his policemen for striking the flag at the station masthead. All three of them were in spotless uniform for the ceremony, and carried out the prescribed drill with the precision of guardsmen on a royal parade. This too, I knew from long experience, was not done for our benefit. The corporal raised and lowered the flag at sunrise and sunset with the same punctilious observance of form throughout the year, whether there was anyone to witness the ceremony or not. It was to him what dressing each night for dinner was to Maugham's lone Englishman on his South Sea island; it kept the desert and the casual ways of its children from invading his spirit, even more effectively than the barbed-wire fence kept the creeping sand and thorn from biting into his compound. Certainly it was most remarkable how the disappearance of one small flag from the immense sky looming over the tiny row of huts made the whole evening for a moment look abandoned and forlorn.

'You ought to have a look at Dabé; he's far from well,' said Ben, who had come out to meet me the moment the ceremony was over.

Alarmed, I accompanied him to one of the huts set aside for us. Dabé was lying on the dung floor, eyes tightly shut, breathing fast and harshly as if his windpipe had contracted. I felt his pulse, which was beating at a fantastic rate. I took his temperature: it was normal. In spite of his terrible labour to get air, and the blankets piled on him, he was not sweating. When I asked him what was wrong, he did not answer. He only opened his eyes wide and gave me a look through which his own darkness poured into me. Suddenly I was back many years in a compound which had been turned into a cage for prisoners of war by the Japanese in Java. There, the evening I was released from confinement in the condemned cell, I was asked to look at an Australian officer. He was sick, in just the way Dabé was sick now, and he gave me the same look. Months afterwards, when we came to a prison with doctors, they said the officer's was a grave case of asthma. For two and a half years they had a tremendous tussle to get adrenalin enough to relieve his attacks, which became more severe and frequent. The strange thing was that the officer had never had an attack of asthma in his life before the evening on which I saw him – his first evening in a Japanese prison. Stranger still, from the moment he was released at the end of the war the attacks vanished and have not returned to this day.

I have always been disposed to take seriously what rises unbidden to the surface of my mind. I had no doubt that this recollec-
tion could not have emerged from the welter of my own past in
prison if Dabé and the officer had not been two of a kind. I have
mentioned Dabé's fear of the outside world. This slight foretaste of
the outside world at Tsane had brought fear back to imprison him
– a fear all the more formidable because it was rooted deep in the
terrible history of extermination of his people. His life, his breath,
he believed, was about to be taken from him. I had no adrenalin,
but I thought that if I could release his spirit, as that officer's spirit
had been when he got out of prison, he would be able to breathe
freely again. All depended on how much he had come to trust me.

So I told him, in the only idiom I thought he would understand,
that an alien spirit had taken hold of him and was trying to harm
him. At that he tried pathetically to raise his head and nod. I said
we would give him powerful medicine and drive the spirit out of
him. The medicine would be in two parts: the first half to make his
own spirit stand up and fight the enemy until it ran away, the
second to make his spirit rest and awake so strong in the morning
that no enemy spirit would venture near him again. We gave him
nearly half a tumbler of old Cognac, sugar, and hot water, and
three Anadins. He swallowed them eagerly, though with difficulty.
Within half an hour his breathing became easier and his wrinkled
old face relaxed. Some two hours later he asked for food: after the
food I gave him a sleeping draught called Nembutal. He examined
the two little capsules against the light of a hurricane lamp, noticing
that one half of each was yellow and the other white. His finger felt
first the yellow and then the white. When he tried to divide the two
with the nail of the finger and failed, he looked enormously pleased.
He smiled and gave me the sideways glance which was always a
sign that I was about to be teased.

'Moren!' he said hoarsely, 'you're more of a skelm than any
spirit.'

At sunrise the next morning I went to see how he was, hoping he
would be well enough for us to start immediately after breakfast.
His bed on the floor was empty, but from behind the hut an extraordinary sound was coming. There was in the wall a square opening
which served as a window, and I went to it at once to see what
caused the sound. It was Dabé, standing sideways on, fully dressed,
his hat in his hand and head turned over his shoulder, eyes fixed on

his own shadow which in that light lay like ink on the crimson sand and stretched to just beyond the far end of the compound. The voice which made the noise was not at all Dabé's normal one but hoarse, oddly authoritative, and deep, as if it came with the beat of an incantation from the pit of his stomach.

'Who is he,' the voice chanted, 'who stands here in the morning sun?

'Who is he with so tall a shadow beside him?

'Whose shadow is this that starts at sunrise and ends at sunset?

'Who is he who travels so far from his shelter and people?

'Who is he who fears neither police nor kaffir nor red stranger?

'Who is he who has an ostrich feather in his hat?

'Who is he who puts the hat on the bare head of the shadow?'

The voice paused while Dabé clamped firmly on his head the ridiculous European hat he insisted on wearing. Then he resumed deeper than ever on a big drum-like note:

'Why, Dabé, you child of a Bushman, you! It is you!' And with that he pranced a sprightly step or two, as a child might on release for play after hours of detention at school.

He could not ever have known how this little shadow show at sunrise moved me. Another memory had come unbidden to my mind, standing there beside him and his shadow. I remembered my mother telling me something about one of the little old Bushmen on my grandfather's farm. He always rode beside the driver on the box of the coach which my grandfather used to take his family to church in town. He was always absorbed watching the shadow of the vehicle and its four spirited horses travel in the dust beside the track, and from time to time he saluted his own little silhouette of shade in the way Dabé had just done, with the same deep ventriloquist's voice, which my mother imitated perfectly. Invariably he ended with the cry:

'Whose feather is that fluttering in the wind over all those shadows in the dust?

'Why, Bushman, it is yours!'

The memory, I am certain, came to reassure me that Dabé was back for the moment in the safe keeping of his own natural spirit. But each night from then on, Dabé came to me for one of the yellow and white sleeping draughts, and always I gave him one.

6 A Bravery of Birds

From Tsane we travelled fast eastwards towards the great pans of Kukong and Kakia along one of the oldest tracks across the desert. At one place where there was unexpectedly good shade in which we paused to rest at noon, Ben said: 'You know, I came by here first as a boy of eight leading the oxen in my father's front wagon. We camped here, and almost at once some Bushmen came to see us. They had their shelters only a hundred yards from here, and came to offer us skins of game in exchange for tobacco. I passed this spot many times afterwards and always they reappeared for the same purpose, friendly, gay, and excited. Ten years ago I came by again, but they had vanished. I was afraid they had died in the outbreak of pest which raged just then in the Kalahari, until I met an old Bushman I knew at the well at Kukong. I asked him, because you know it is amazing how they pass on news of one another from end to end of the desert. He seemed astonished that I had not heard of so shocking an event. Did I not know, he asked, that they had heard people passing along the track one day and rushed out as they always did to barter their skins? Well, the government was travelling by, and when the police with the government saw that among the skins there was one of a gemsbuck, they took the two best young hunters away with them. The remaining people immediately moved right away from the tracks. They were safe all right, but their hearts were troubled for the two young men who had not come back, as the hearts of all the people had been wide open to the young men. As you see, the Bushmen are not back on their ancient stand and will, I fear, never be again.'

'But why did the police do that?' someone asked.

'Because the gemsbuck is royal game here and protected,' Ben said, his voice edged with the irony of it, 'and the Bushman is not.'

'What happened to the two young hunters? Do you know?' I asked.

He shook his head sadly, saying he could only guess they had never returned because once such essentially innocent people had been punished and imprisoned they became so deeply confused that they seldom found the way back.

The same evening, camp made earlier than usual because of good progress that day, Ben and I took our guns to see if we could not shoot a springbuck for our supper and breakfast. We found some in a pan near by, but they were on the other side – too far for us to

Gemsbuck: royal game

stalk effectively before dark. The moment we set foot on the floor of the pan they were aware of us, stopped grazing, and stood heads up to watch us apprehensively. So we started to climb back on to the ridge overlooking the pan with the idea of sitting down there for a while to enjoy the stillness and beauty of the evening.

The end of the journey was very near now. It is remarkable how a sense of valediction heightens one's awareness of the beauty of the world: I think it is because beauty is a summons to journey, is both a hail and a farewell of the spirit, and since our deepest pattern is a round of departure and return, we never recognize it more clearly than at the beginning and end of our journeys. Indeed all the traffic and the travail in between may be directed just to that end. Besides, when one has lived as close to nature for as long as we had done, one is not tempted to commit the metropolitan error of assuming that the sun rises and sets, the day burns out and the night falls, in a world outside oneself. These are great and reciprocal events, which occur also in ourselves. In this moment of heightened sensibility, there on the lip of the pan like words never before spoken, I was convinced that, just as the evening was happening in us, so were we in it, and the music of our participation in a single overwhelming event was flowing through us.

This sense of participation enclosed in one moment of time was increased by the presence of the pan itself. From the ridge where we seated ourselves we had an immense view of the desert. In that light it looked in terms of earth what the sea is in terms of water – without permanent form and without end. Then suddenly there was the pan at our feet, a shape which was definite and real, the ridge describing an almost perfect circle against the sky and presenting the waste around it with a flawless container. It was a geometrical paradigm of life's need for form, a demonstration of the proposition that unless life were contained it could not be. I remembered the excitement I felt on first seeing an Etruscan vase, perceiving why the summons for a renewal of the European spirit had to emerge in men's imagination as a vision of a greater container in the shape of the Holy Grail. But I got no further, for just then Ben interrupted. He asked, in a voice so much affected by the mood of the moment that it was barely more than a whisper: 'Do you remember this place?'

'I do, Ben.' I recognized it as country we had passed through several times before, but no more. Knowing from his tone he had something particular in mind, I said: 'Why did you ask?'

'Because of the ostriches. We saw them first just by those bushes there. Surely you remember them?' He sounded somewhat disappointed at my vague response.

But I had it now! The pan was the scene of one of the loveliest deeds I have ever seen. Nearly ten years ago, Ben and I had come fast over the ridge one evening and without pause slipped down the side silently in our truck. As a result we surprised what looked like a lone couple of ostriches on the edge of the floor of the pan. The birds had panicked; they circled each other wildly until a clear design of action emerged. To our amazement the female broke away from her mate and came resolutely towards us. Ben, who was driving, halted the truck at once and said: 'Please, don't move! Just watch this.'

Knowing how ostriches hate and fear men, I do not think I have ever seen a braver deed. The bird was desperately afraid. Her heart beating visibly in her throat, she advanced towards us like a soldier against a machine-gun post. With the late afternoon sun making a halo round her feathers, which stood erect with the fearful tension in her, she came on, pretending to be mortally hurt, limping badly and trailing one great wing as if it were broken. Then, trying to give the impression that she had only just seen us, she stopped, whisked about and skipped with broken steps sideways into the bush. Before she had gone far, however, she halted. The one great wing sagged more than ever, giving her a list like a ship about to founder. She looked fearfully over her shoulder to see if we were following her. When she saw we had not done so, she appeared baffled and dismayed, and once more came back towards us to repeat the performance, this time so close that the trailing wing nearly touched the bumper of the truck.

Meanwhile the male, in the shining black dress of a bountiful summer, hurried the other way in a zigzag fashion like a ship tacking into the wind. He would rush off in a few giant strides, stop,

An eagle

lower his head, flap his wings, look up to see how the female was getting on, then run off on the other tack again. When his rushes had presently taken him into a bare patch of sand higher up on the ridge, we saw the cause of it all: the male was trying to hustle out of danger nineteen little ostrich chickens, while the female distracted our attention by doing all she could to entice us into capturing her instead. The chickens were so new that the sheen of the yolk of the eggs from which they had been hatched was like silk upon them. All the time they were within sight their mother became increasingly reckless in her efforts to draw us away, and once she looked truly tragic with despair because we would not follow her. Not until her family was out of sight did she desist: even then she did not hasten to join them, but with her wing still trailing drew away from us in the opposite direction. How could I not remember?

I looked at the place where it had all happened, and in the light of the memory it looked like hallowed ground. I think Ben felt something similar, because he began speaking to me with a release of emotion he rarely allowed himself. And I report his words here in full because they helped me greatly later in understanding the imagery of birds in the first spirit of things.

People, he said, often asked him which of all the creatures encountered in his many years as a hunter and dweller in far-away places of Africa, he found most impressive. Always he answered that it would have to be a bird of some kind. This never failed to surprise them, because people are apt to be dazzled by physical power, size, frightfulness, and they expected him to say an elephant, lion, buffalo, or some other imposing animal. But he stuck to his answer; there was nothing more wonderful in Africa than its birds. I asked why precisely. He paused and drew a circle with his finger in the red sand in front of him before saying that it was for many reasons, but in the first place because birds flew. He said it in such a way that I felt I had never before experienced fully the wonder of birds flying.

I waited silently for him to find the next link in his chain of thought. In the second place, he remarked, because birds sang. He himself loved all natural sounds in the bush and the desert, but he had to admit none equalled the sounds of birds. It was as if the sky made music in their throats and one could hear the sun rise and set, the night fall and the first stars come out in their voices. Other animals were condemned to make only such noises as they must, but birds seemed free to utter the sounds they wanted to, to shape them at will and invent new ones to express all the emotions of living matter released on wings from its own dead weight. He knew of nothing so beautiful as the sight of a bird utterly abandoned to its song, every bit of its being surrendered to the music, the tip of the tiniest feather trembling like a tuning-fork with sound. And sometimes even they danced to their own music. But they not only sang. They also conversed. There appeared to be little they could not convey to one another by sound. He himself had always listened with the greatest care to bird sound and never ceased to marvel at the variety of intelligence it conveyed to him.

Old-fashioned stork

Stranger still was their capacity of being aware of things before they happened. This was positively amazing. When the great earth tremor shook the northern Kalahari some years before, Ben was travelling with a herd of cattle along the fringes of the Okovango swamp. One day he was watching some old-fashioned storks, sacred ibis, and giant herons along the edges of a stream. Suddenly the birds stopped feeding, looked uneasily about them, and then all at once took to their wings as if obedient to a single command. They rose quickly into the air and began wheeling over the river, making the strangest sounds. The sound had not fallen long on the still air before the ground under his feet started to shake, the cattle to bellow and run, and as far as his eyes could see the banks of the stream began to break away from the bush as if sliced from it by a knife and to collapse into the water. He had no doubt the birds knew what was coming, and he made a careful note of their behaviour and the sound they uttered.

Even more wonderful, however, was their beauty. Colour, for instance, lovely as it was in most animals, served the latter only for camouflage. But with birds it was much more. Of all the creatures, none dressed so well as the birds of Africa. They had summer and winter dresses, special silks for making love, coats and skirts for travel, and more practical clothes that did not show the dirt and

Secretary-bird

wear and tear of domestic use. Even the soberest ones among them, which went about the country austere as elders of the Dutch Reformed Church collecting from parsimonious congregations on Sunday mornings – the old-fashioned storks in black and white, or the secretary-birds with their stiff starched fronts and frock coats – their dress was always of an impeccable taste.

This beauty and good taste did not stop at dress. It showed in the building of their nests: no animals could rival the diversity and elegance of the homes birds made for themselves. The worst builders were the carnivorous ones – the toughy-pants like the lamb-catchers, batteleurs, and white-breasted jackal birds. Just as the warrior races in Africa built the worst huts in the land, so did the fighting birds make the ugliest homes; but on the whole the nests of the birds were things of beauty and joy.

Most wonderful of all was the way this beauty appeared in their eggs – shaped and painted as if by an artist. Had I ever seen a bird's egg that was ugly? Compare these lovely speckled, dappled, or sky-blue surfaces, slightly milky as if veiled by a remote cirrus cloud, to the eggs laid by snakes, turtles, and crocodiles. Even the drabbest of eggs laid by a bird was beautiful in comparison. Ben himself was always excited when a mere farmyard hen produced eggs with a gipsy tan and tiny sun-freckles on the shell. Again, birds

'*The worst builders were the carnivorous ones . . .*'

collaborated, in forethought and purpose, with other living creatures. There was the bird that picked the crocodile's teeth clean for him; the bird that rode the rhinoceros, feeding on the parasites that troubled him and warning him of danger in return for his hospitality; the egret who did the same for cattle and buffalo; and perhaps the greatest of them all, the honey-diviner who, as I had seen for myself, even co-operated with the universally feared and mistrusted man.

Finally there was their quality of courage. I had witnessed an example of it that day years ago in a female ostrich; but all birds had it. When one considered what tender, small, delicate, and defenceless things most birds were, they were perhaps the bravest creatures in the world. He had seen far more moving instances of the courage of the birds of Africa than he could possibly relate, but he would mention only one of the most common – birds defending their nests against snakes. On those occasions they had a rallying cry, which was a mixture of faith and courage, just keeping ahead of despair and fear. It would draw birds from all round to the point of danger, and the recklessness with which one little feathered body after another would hurl itself at the head of a snake, beating with its wings and shrieking its valkyrie cry, had to be seen to be believed. Ben once saw a black mamba driven dazed out of a tree by only a score or so of resolute little birds. The mamba, which he killed, measured close on ten feet, and this snake is itself a creature of fiery courage and determination. No, all in all, he had no doubt that birds were the most wonderful of all living things.

Ben paused, and motioned to me to listen. The first of the night plovers was calling from the far end of the pan, a long sort of wail like a ship's pipe mustering her crew to take her out to sea. It was nearly dark. I had not noticed the quick flight of time, so absorbed had I been in listening. When the plover's call died away, Ben jumped to his feet with a cat-like ease that never failed to astonish me in so big a man and asked with one of his rare smiles, had I not heard the referee's whistle? Light, he said, had stopped play. The game was over and it was time to get back to camp.

7 'Go in Peace, Moren'

The next morning Ben reminded me of my promise that I would let him push on ahead when the right moment came. He was sorry, but he felt it was upon him now. The rains were coming up fast on our heels and he must get back to plough his long-suffering earth. So that very afternoon, a mile or so beyond the first pan after Kakia, we made our earliest camp yet. While Ben and the others unloaded his vehicle, so that he could forge on fast all through the night, I took my gun and walked with Dabé back to the pan. I had seen a flicker of springbuck there as we passed. I badly wanted to give Ben something there and then as a token of what his help and example had meant to me. I wanted to do it all the more because of a feeling that this might be our last moment ever in the desert to-gether: I had no doubt I would return; but I was not sure that, by the time I could, it would be right to ask Ben to accompany me again. He was a good deal older than I. Fit as he was, I had been anxious at times about the signs of physical strain in him of the long journey behind us. He, Vyan, and I had gone on several expeditions into the unknown parts of the desert. The thought that the three of us might never again do another Kalahari journey together was hard to accept, but I found some relief in this search for something to give him before he left. There was nothing where we were, I felt, more suitable than a hunter's gift of the buck, which is one of the greatest of the natural delicacies of Africa.

Fortunately the vivid springbuck were still in the pan. It is true they were far away and right out in the open where it was impossible to stalk them; but the light of the sun was behind me and for the moment they were standing still in it, gold and brown, only their outlines trembling slightly like shapes seen through the tranquil water of a coral lagoon. I lay down on the edge of the pan, Dabé standing beside me dubiously shaking his head over the long, lucid, trembling distance. I aimed my gun and shot quickly. It is odd how much better one shoots when one is not shooting for oneself. The leading ram instantly fell over on his side and lay still. It was 450 paces from where I shot to where we picked him up, a bullet through his heart. He was so heavy that Dabé and I got him back to camp only with great difficulty, arriving exhausted just in time, for Ben was waiting only on my return to go. From the look he gave me, I believe the gift conveyed what I had hoped it would.

That night too we heard our last lion. He was just at the right distance from us to make the sound of his roar perfect. I have always been grateful that I was born into a world and shall die in one where the lion, however diminished in number, is still roaring. Heard in his and my native setting, it is for me the most beautiful sound in the world. It is to silence what the shooting star is to the dark of the night. All that black night long the roar of the lion came and went around our camp, and ceased finally only at dawn. The

A lion's spoor by a wild sisal plant

spoor of the lion by the first sunlight was one of the biggest any of us had ever seen, and completely circled our fire.

The evening of that day we ourselves reached the fringes of the permanently settled part of the southern Kalahari. Two days later we were back where we had started from in the village of Lobatsi, which lies hard by the meeting-place on the foothills of the great central plateau of Africa and the far eastern limit of the Kalahari. There we began at once the dreary task of winding up the expedition. What we had left of supplies we distributed among our African companions. We made haste to reserve seats in the first train to the Victoria Falls for Vyan and his Knipsigis bearer, Cheruyiot – or 'Jambo' as he was affectionately known to everyone. From there they would still have in front of them a journey by truck of some thousands of miles back to East Africa, where Vyan was long overdue. I paid off those who had come for hire and gave them as generous a bonus as I could possibly afford, because they had served us all well and for far longer than I had engaged them.

When all the details connected with such an undertaking had been settled, and everyone was free to go his individual way, I noticed again that marked reluctance to do so which seizes the heart at the end of a journey. It is as if an instinct warns one of the capacity of the familiar world to kill an experience it has not shared. I thought of people who had been prisoners of war with me and who for three and a half years had longed for the day of return home. Yet when the moment of release came, they were almost paralysed with reluctance. Scores of them wrote back to me in Java that once safe in London they could not bear to disperse. They moved around the city in packs, eating together at the same places and sleeping whenever possible at the same lodgings. One friend even, in despair after a fortnight spent thus, had to go up to a policeman and, giving him the address of his parents in Sussex, beg the man to take him home because he could not do so himself. Something of the same subtle fear now was active among my companions. I had to get Charles and Duncan to drive, almost by force, first John to his home and then Jeremiah back to his wife and that 'very, very clever son' of his whose snapshot I knew by heart in all its faded and much-fingered detail.

The one exception was Dabé, who was in a fever to go. I myself relished so little the imminent parting that the egoist in me was somewhat put out by his eagerness to get back to his desert home. But then I had to admit that our situations were not comparable: we were at the end of our desert journey, facing a world which would feel indifference for what we had been to one another; Dabé was in a world which despised what he was in himself, and he was only half-way through his travels. Besides, he was as excited as a child because he was going most of the way back by train.

He had never seen trains before, let alone travelled in one, and when not busy with us he stood for hours at the entrance of the provincial commissioner's home where we were staying, waiting for a train to come by. The main line to the Rhodesias, which skirts the Kalahari for some five hundred miles, passed by a bare eighty yards from the gate. At first when a train appeared in the pass in the hills, shrieking at the top of its whistle at the little Lobatsi station and blowing out steam and smoke from the effort of hauling itself up the gradient and over the saddle in the gap, Dabé would begin to tremble just like a little boy seeing his first express engine rushing towards a country platform. When the train was immediately opposite the gate, he could bear his emotions no longer and would throw himself flat on the lawn behind the trim hedge which protected the lovely little garden against the dust. But soon he mastered himself enough to watch the train until it came screaming to a halt in the station. When that first happened he tripped the sprightly little steps I had first seen at Tsane, chanting in his ventriloquist's voice:

'Who is he who stands without fear watching the span of iron oxen bellowing by?

'Who is he whose "Hokai"* makes the runaway wagon halt?

'Why Dabé, you child of a Bushman you! It is you.'

Ironically, such fear as remained was mine, and I was made acutely aware of it within a few hours of our arrival in Lobatsi. I had gone to Lobatsi station, taking both Cheruyiot and Dabé with me. By force of the circumstances of the crazy mixed-up history of Africa, although Lobatsi was in a British Protectorate the railway itself belonged to Southern Rhodesia and yet was operated by the Union Government. The staff at the Lobatsi railway station, therefore, was South African. On our arrival I left Dabé and Cheruyiot walking up and down the platform, their little fingers hooked together and conversing in a language they had evolved in the course of the journey out of a little Swahili, some Sechuana and a lot of onomatopoeia. I was nearing the end of a long conversation in the office about an expensive parcel that had gone astray months before when I heard a voice saying loudly in English, with a marked South African accent: 'I trust the two gentlemen are comfortable. Is there perhaps some little something I could do to make them more comfortable? Would the gentlemen not perhaps like a glass of wine and a cigar or two?'

The words themselves could not have been more affable, but the tone in which they were uttered was as friendly as a ring-necked cobra's hiss. Breaking off my conversation, I hurried outside to

* Common African wagoner's exhortation used to halt his team of oxen.

see Dabé and Cheruyiot seated on one of the station benches and the stationmaster, white with anger, bowing with mock obsequiousness to them. The expressions on their faces were of utter bewilderment. Tired of walking about, they had done the most natural thing in the world – seated themselves on an empty bench on an empty platform. They could not know that they had transgressed a great though unwritten law of the station and done what no other black or coloured person would have dared to do. The bench was reserved for Europeans.

What made the stationmaster angrier than ever was the fact that the law against their behaviour was unwritten: it had come about purely by that subtle process of induction with which the terrible charge of colour prejudice in South Africa projects its sombre electricity into the atmosphere of all the neighbouring territories. Although Lobatsi was in British territory, where racial discrimination is not legal and the railway benches – unlike those in the Union – are not lettered for 'Europeans' or 'Non-Europeans', the presence of a South African staff who were close to their own country had been enough to make discrimination even on this remote little station an iron fact of normal life. Neither Dabé nor Cheruyiot understood a single word of English; they remained seated, gaping at the official. He was getting still angrier at what he obviously regarded as dumb insolence; where it would have ended I do not know, because I stopped it. Giving him some of his own medicine, I said: 'How very charming of you! They have come a long way across the desert and I am certain would love a glass of wine and a cigar.'

He whipped around as if a bee had stung him, exclaiming: 'My God! My God!' Shaking with unbelief as well as anger, he looked me up and down, then spluttered: 'Are they yours?'

'They work for me, if that is what you mean,' I answered.

'My God!' he said again, putting his hands to his head with the melodrama of despair. 'My God! One of those!' With that he walked down the line towards some points, where he slammed the lever over with such force that it was a wonder the track did not come apart. As he did so the scream of the engine which had brought him out of his office broke from the pass and an enormous black goods train came thundering towards us. It was Dabé's first train. I was still wondering how to explain the incident to him and Cheruyiot, but one glance up the line was too much for him.

He vanished with unbelievable speed, dashing for the station exit and disappearing a hundred yards away through the gate in the provincial commissioner's garden, a veil of red dust hanging in the air over his beeline into cover.

From that moment I had grave misgivings about the wisdom of allowing Dabé to go home most of the way by train. It meant that from Lobatsi he would have to travel deep into the Union to a place called De Aar (the artery), change there in the middle of the night, spend several more days in a South African train to Windhoek, change again for Gobabis to catch the fortnightly mail truck to Ghanzis, and so by degrees back to his home near Gemsbok Pan. The incident on Lobatsi station had shown me the danger to which he would be exposed for most of the journey, and I was troubled by a vision of Dabé thrown in gaol for having transgressed in all his innocence one of the laws of South Africa's colour ethic. If that happened, I was certain the shock could easily be the end of him: he might die in an acute fit of breathlessness such as that which had so alarmed us at Tsane.

It had never been our intention to send him on that complicated and protracted railway journey home. We had known that one of the foremost ranchers near Gemsbok Pan was in the Union and coming back by truck across the desert. An old friend, we were certain he would take Dabé back with him. Unfortunately our journey out lasted longer than we expected, so we missed him by three days. Dabé refused to wait for another opportunity, which might not come for weeks. He insisted on going by train; and once he had mastered his fear of passing trains, he was more determined than ever to get inside them.

I talked the problem over with the provincial commissioner, to whose counsel and friendship we owed much. He was highly indignant about the incident on the station, and not at all inclined to treat it lightly. He said he would have up the stationmaster and draft instructions to ensure that the station was run in the spirit as well as the letter of Protectorate law. Nonetheless, he thought, we could organize Dabé's journey in such a way that he ran no risk. To this end, he drafted on government paper, carrying his most imposing seal, a letter to all officials Dabé might encounter on his way, stating that he was travelling in the service of the administration of the Protectorate and exhorting them to help him to his destination. He was certain Dabé would only have to produce the letter whenever he was in doubt or trouble to get all the assistance he needed. Then he undertook to put Dabé into his train and instruct the conductor to see him through what would be the most critical phase of his journey, the night change at Die Aar. I myself gave Dabé a letter to someone I knew in the frontier township of Gobabis, with the request to look after him until the truck to Ghanzis left. I enclosed also a liberal cheque for expenses, and asked him to send me a telegram when Dabé arrived and another when he was on the last lap home. Thereafter we drilled Dabé thoroughly in what he had to do. This, since he was a person of natural intelligence, was not at all difficult.

So the days at Lobatsi vanished, with terrifying speed. I was parting from people who meant much to me and with some of whom, like Vyan, I had bonds that went back a long way into closely-shared experience. Yet the prospect of parting with them affected me less deeply than that of parting with Dabé. The turmoil of my feelings about him was so great that no explanation available to me would wholly account for it. It certainly was not the length of time I had known him, because compared to my relationships with other members of the expedition, ours was the briefest of all. It was not because I knew him well: I realized that I had touched only the outskirts of his personality. Yet slight as was my conscious knowledge of him, intuitively there had grown up a strong recognition. The main emotion, perhaps, spread from there and was certainly fed by a feeling that in our brief encounter with his people in the desert we had been freed for a moment from the negations of the past and recaptured a child-like innocence in ourselves. We had shared a fleeting glimpse of history as I knew in my heart of hearts it could and should have been, and with our going now were saying good-bye not merely to a rediscovered childhood but to all life itself when young.

To what extent he was aware of this I could not tell and made no effort to discover. I believe it is ignoble to inflict on others feelings they cannot possibly understand. I could only hope that, when Dabé was no longer distracted like a young boy in a Christmas Day nursery by the twentieth-century world around him, he would on looking back over the journey find some warmth and light to cheer him in the cold dark denial of his being that awaited him when he returned to his life with masters who despised the Bushman and his ways. But what interested me more than my own feelings were signs that everyone else shared them in a measure. They vied with one another to press gifts on Dabé. Even Jeremiah, who had remained most aloof from him, gave him a pipe and tobacco, and instead of calling him 'you' as he had done ever since I forbade him the inflammatory epithet of 'Massarwa', took him by the wrist, and, using his name for the first time since they had met, said: 'Good-bye, Dabé.' In the end the suitcase and duffel bag we had given Dabé were nearly bursting with presents, and his pockets crackling with notes of money.

On the morning of the eve of his departure he accompanied me to the station for the last time. He was dressed in going-away clothes of his own choosing. On his feet he had a pair of elegant brown suede ankle-boots, with white tennis socks reaching to his calves. His khaki shorts, a little too long, were fastened with a Boy Scout belt, the buckle of which displayed above his navel the motto 'Be Prepared'. He wore a spotless white shirt, open at the neck, and on his head a little green pork-pie hat with his imposing ostrich feather stuck in the side. From behind, his figure looked like that of a not fully grown boy – an orphan perhaps, hurriedly fitted out at some charitable jumble sale. It was only from in front and by looking at his finely creased old face and deep into those eyes of his that one had some idea of the years and the fire wherein his spirit had burned. When I gave him his ticket he remarked portentously that there was one important thing I had forgotten: his medicine, those little white and yellow pills. I gave him eight. I would gladly have given him more, but I was afraid that in a moment of panic, when an invasion of foreign spirits appeared imminent to him, he might swallow the lot. He promised me he would never take more than one a night and pleaded for more. I insisted that eight taken one at a time would see him to Gobabis and out of danger of invasion, and refused to give him more. With that he poured the capsules into an empty canvas tobacco bag, which he tied securely to his Boy Scout belt.

I wanted to see him into his train myself, but if I were to get to Table Bay in time for my ship, I could not delay any more. So I said good-bye to him at noon in the yard of the provincial commissioner's house, which has been open to me as often as if it were my own home. As I was driving through the gate, he reappeared running at the window by my side. I stopped immediately.

'Yes, Dabé?' I asked.

'Moren. Please, what is the time?' he replied anxiously.

I am not certain what I had expected but it was certainly not that question.

'It's five past twelve,' I told him. 'You need not worry. You have hours before your train.'

'Auck! Moren,' he exclaimed, no sooner put out than recovered. 'You are really a great skelm.'

He paused, turned his head to stare deep into the great summer's day, before remarking quietly as if to himself: 'What am I to do without you, to know the things I think before I know them myself? Go in peace, Moren!'

He was still standing drenched in sun at the gate when I stopped some distance down the road to fasten a flap which had been overlooked. It was too far to tell whether he was watching me out of sight or waiting for another train. It is frightening how swiftly separation achieves its purpose. The journey, I told myself, was finally and irrevocably over, and yet I was to find that in a sense it had hardly begun.

Part Two: World Between

'Pitié pour nous qui combattons toujours aux frontières
De l'illimité et de l'avenir.

GUILLAUME APOLLINAIRE

8 Time of the Hyena

I kept my promise to Dabé to speak to the government in Mafe-king. It was not, of course, as he had informed me, an old gentle-man with a white beard. Even its chief representative responsible for the administration of the Protectorate was not old, but young and new to the post. I had met him before in other roles on other missions to southern Africa and was not afraid that his mind would be sealed in advance to the issue I had to raise.

He listened patiently, attentively, and with growing sympathy while I told him something of the story of the Bushman as I have told it in *The Lost World of the Kalahari*. I stressed that it would be a terrible mistake to assume that the process of thousands of years of extermination of the Bushman, which I described there, was ended. It might not be quite so obvious and brutal, but it went on still in a subtle way. In fact, even some of the old-fashioned methods against the Bushman were still used from time to time. Did he know, for instance, that the despotic Bamangwato, who were so efficient at soliciting sympathy from Britain for their own causes, had for years called up Impis regularly and sent them on expeditions across the north-west frontiers of their reserve in the Kalahari, against the Bushman, on the pretext that he had raided their cattle outposts? Did he know how the Bamangwato and other 'Chuana tribes took the Bushman's women at will and made slaves of him and his children? If he looked into these things, he would still find all over Bechuanaland something of the same historic pattern of extermination which had gradually destroyed the Bushman all along the expanding frontiers of the black dominions in the north and the white colony in the south of Africa.

But far more important to my mind was the fact that mere con-tact with twentieth-century life seemed lethal to the Bushman. He was essentially so innocent and natural a person that he had only to come near us for a sort of radioactive fall-out from our unnatural world to produce a fatal leukaemia in his spirit. The Bushman himself was instinctively aware of the danger and tried to keep away, but that was becoming more and more difficult. He sought shelter as always in the desert, but there was no place there which he could call strictly his own. The invaders of his territory in the Kalahari all had reserves – vast areas recognized and protected by law, enforceable rights and representation, but he had none. He who once was lord and master of it all, owned nothing in it today, possessed not even the licence to hunt freely for survival in it. I recited all the instances Dabé had given me, added others supplied by Tom Hardbattle, and several from my own experience. I told him about the Bushman community that had disappeared on the way to Kakia because his police had taken two of the hunters away for killing a gemsbuck.

If he still doubted the Bushman's fear of our world and our laws, I begged him to consider the murder of some R.A.F. men in the northern Kalahari some years before. They had made a forced landing in the desert and were trying to reach Francistown on foot when they met a group of Bushmen in the bush. The Bushmen fed them and sheltered them in the night.

The episode had been presented to the world as a typical example of Bushman treachery and brutality. But I had heard it from the Bushman's side. It was fear of the deepest kind that had driven them to it. They had just killed a giraffe for food – and a giraffe in that area was a protected animal. When the R.A.F. men suddenly appeared in their midst in uniforms, they concluded, since the only uniforms they knew were always worn by police, that they were police come to investigate the killing of the giraffe. They feared that as a result some of them were to be taken away never to return; all night long while their guests slept they debated what to do. In the end they decided reluctantly that as a matter of survival they had to kill the men. We and the law itself were the main accessories before the fact of murder.

It did not help that such laws were made with good intentions. Not long before, I had been discussing the Bushman with a public-spirited and dedicated district commissioner. The 'D.C.' was proud of the fact that he had just levied a tax on all Bushmen encountered in his area. The tax, he was convinced, would make 'useful citizens' of the Bushmen by forcing them to work for the ranchers in his district in order to earn the money to pay the tax.

'I will teach them,' he told me, warm in his faith in the virtue of his decree, 'not to lead such feckless, useless lives.' Yet it was a terribly inhuman thing to do to such a person as the Bushman, who has no conception of money, tax, property, and what we call work, and who had never been consulted before the passing of the law. In a gaol in a Kalahari outpost I had seen some of the Bushmen convicted of failure to pay the tax. They had no idea what they had done wrong. They just looked as if the last light in their hearts had been put out, and as if they would soon become not useful but dead citizens.

When the administrator raised an eyebrow at the phrase 'dead citizens', I assured him it was not exaggerated. For the Bushman, life was movement: when the freedom to move was taken from him, life itself tended to cease. I knew of one Bushman, committed to gaol for an offence against a game law, who had died for no other reason than confinement. No, I certainly could not agree that the look in the eyes of the Bushman convicts I had just seen on my way through the desert was the best a British administration could do.

Meanwhile, what happened to the women and children of these little men suddenly put into convicts' suits? Life was hard enough with the hunter free to find food for them, but without him it became almost impossible. Tom Hardbattle, who knew most about the Bushman trapped on the fringes of the Bantu and European encroachment in the Kalahari, had told me grim stories of their plight, which I now repeated. As I did so, the ghost of one woman suddenly deprived in this manner of her hunter came into my mind.

She had followed her man to the gaol at Gemsbok Pan where he was imprisoned, and there had been forced to live on such scraps of charity as the outpost could afford. The black and coloured men who came and went as drovers, lorry-boys, and servants of white buyers and traders, took her at their will, throwing her some tobacco or food in return. How long it all had gone on I could not tell, because the first time I saw her, life in its ultimate mercy had already deprived her of her senses. One white morning she walked by my camp at Gemsbok Pan stark naked, beating her chest and moaning pitifully. Bushman women wear little enough, but when they discard that little it is a sure sign they are divesting themselves of all relationship with the outside world, as it would be if a woman tore off her clothes in Piccadilly in the middle of the day.

113

I had called Dabé and asked what was wrong with her. He used a phrase Bushmen use when disaster has come to the soul: 'The time of the hyena is upon her.' We went after her. Overtaken, she turned on us, seeing without seeing, whimpering like an abandoned puppy. We took her by the wrists. Gently, making all sorts of cradle-side noises to comfort her, we led her back to camp while the few outpost loafers looking on laughed – not, I am sure, out of cruelty, but because only thus could they endure the accusation against us all implicit in such a sight. We gave her a mug of sweet tea and some food. The first sip of the tea quietened her, as if it proved that, for all the bitterness of her spirit, something sweet was still left in her. Then we clothed her in pants and a shirt of mine that came to her knees. Until we left some hours later, she stayed there fingering the clothes in a wondering, unbelieving manner. Afterwards I was not certain that it had been kind to do what I had done. Could a single moment of atonement do more against so long and bitter a past and so empty a future than throw them in starker relief? But whether it was right or not then, the vision of her plight urged me on.

I returned to the dangers in any official policy for making 'useful citizens' out of the Bushman. Our own civilization was already in danger itself, because we valued people more for the use we could make of them than for what they were in themselves. If my friend had read his paper that morning, he would have seen a decision taken in Johannesburg as a result, I feared, of something I had written about the wonderful eyesight of the Bushmen – to fly some of them from the Kalahari and try them out as sorters of ore on the gold mines.* That was typical: no one seemed to ask himself what sort of a person the Bushman was and what would be the effect on him of being used in such specialized ways.

My friend interrupted me to ask – not, I believe, because he wanted to be difficult but because he was searching for the answer – if the Bushman had no use in the world of our day, if he contributed nothing to society and paid no taxes and did not work, what possible justification could there be for the great expense of effort and money it would take to preserve him. I said that all over Africa we were beginning to realize how, unless we protected the natural life of the continent, it would soon vanish. Even here in the

* The Johannesburg Chamber of Mines to their everlasting credit has since then prohibited all recruiting of Bushmen.

Kalahari his predecessors had found it necessary to protect the eland, giraffe, gemsbok, giant bustard, and other animals and birds because they were threatened with extinction. No one asked what use they were to society, and quite rightly. The answer was self-evident. They were part of the natural fullness of the life of our continent; though no price tag could be put on them, we knew our lives would be immeasurably poorer without them. This applied even to the most destructive of our animals. For example, take the wild dog, which the great-hearted Ben hated so much for its ruthless ways with the gentle quadrupeds of the land: I would lament

Hunting dog

its going, because with it would vanish a beauty of movement never attained by any other creature on earth.

How then could we deny to the Bushman, putting the case at its lowest, what we conceded to the fauna of the land? His was, perhaps, the oldest form of human life left on earth, and our lives would be poorer without it. I asked my companion if he had read about the revival of the theory of a great lost city of stone buried in the Kalahari, and the recent expeditions to discover its site. He had, and wanted to know if I believed in it. I said I did and I did not: I was interested not so much in the lost city as in what made it necessary for people living near the desert to believe there had been a city there once. It was rather like flying saucers to me: I believed in them, not as physical objects sent from outer space to observe us, but as significant events – prophetic portents almost – in the mind of contemporary man. However, all that aside, did he not find it strange that so much energy should be directed at uncovering problematical ruins in order to know what early man was like, when the oldest man of all, older than any ruin of stone, was living comparatively intact in the Kalahari?

I told him about the scientists who had begged to come with me, some because they wanted to measure Bushman heads and behinds, others to measure his sexual organs, others to study his family relationships, and one to analyse his spit; but when I asked them if they were not interested in the Bushman's mind and spirit, in the man as a living whole, they replied: 'That is not our department of science.' We seemed to have destroyed the Bushman without ever bothering to find out what sort of person he really was. I asked my friend if he realized that, in the whole of his administration which governed that vast protectorate, there was not a single official who spoke Bushman language?

What, he asked then, would I advise him to do? Stop immediately, I begged him, all further encroachment in the parts of the Kalahari where the Bushman still had a way of life of his own. The pressure to open up the great Crown lands of the Kalahari to European settlement was certain to increase. I myself had abetted it unwittingly by surveys for economic development in Bechuanaland, which today I regretted. I begged him to resist all such pressure and meanwhile appoint an officer whose task it would be to learn Bushman, to get to know him and his problems. As his knowledge of the Bushman increased, he would see more clearly than we what should be done. What was left of the ancient way of Bushman life in the Kalahari must be imperilled no more: let the Bushman have a corner entirely his own in the Africa that had once been all his. Provided these conditions were established at once, there would still be time to work out the right solution for the future.

Meanwhile I would go to England to complete the film we had just made in the Kalahari. I hoped it would help. It had already slipped into its own natural shape in my mind: I would tell the story of the Bushman as I had told it to my companion, ending with the same appeal I had made to him. I had immense faith in the British people and in the quality of most of the men serving in his administration. There is not another people in the history of the world which has been less corrupted by great power than the British, in spite of the poor view they themselves take of their own imperial past. They possess a capacity for self-criticism unequalled in any other nation, and a sense of decency so imaginative and searching that less scrupulous opponents in the modern world have frequently used it as a weapon against them. I was certain that these things I had described only happened because neither the British people nor the Protectorate administration had had their eyes opened to them. What I could only define as a curious 'black-out' in the spirit of the white man had prevented him from seeing the horror of the Bushman's plight. The problem was increased because in this respect the vision of the black man was even more clouded than the white's. But I was confident that, once the people in Britain realized all these facts, something would be done about the Bushman. I wanted to do all I could by showing my film, by writing about the Bushman and speaking to my friends in Parliament.

I shall always be profoundly grateful to my companion for promptly proving how right I had been in my belief. One of his first acts in his new position was to appoint an officer charged with the duty of learning Bushman and occupying himself with the Bushmen of the Protectorate and their needs. As for the British public, its response was overwhelming; the last episode of the series of six in which the film was shown on B.B.C. television attracted an audience which had been exceeded, I believe, only by the crowds who watched the Coronation of the Queen on their television screens. If it had been money I needed for the Bushman, I could have raised many thousands. It took me nearly a year to reply to all the people who wrote to me. The whole film was shown a second time, and keeps on reappearing in shortened versions for schools. Even in Canada and Australia it evoked similar reactions. In due course, too, the appropriate questions were asked in Parliament and the official machine set working on behalf of the Bushman at last.

Even I myself was not naïve enough to think it could be left at that. I knew the Bushman would not be safe until he was taken into our hearts and imagination as well, and so into our vision of the future. That meant exacting work of quite a different kind; but on that summer's afternoon in Mafeking I did not know even this much. I had only my own belief that something like this could be done. Against it, I was conscious of a host of obvious negative factors, such as the obstinate tradition of denial of the Bushman all over southern Africa both black and white, and the difficulty of making a modern government take specific action, which only those who have ever attempted the task can realize.

Also, my own tools just then looked hardly adequate. I myself was only too well aware of the shortcomings of my film material. It was not at all what I had hoped to bring back. Almost everything that could go wrong had gone wrong on the journey behind me. At one moment it looked as if I would have to return to England without any film of the Bushman at all. When finally we did encounter a small community of Bushmen, we had to work against time: the surest way to court failure and disaster in Africa is to be in a hurry. I had not been surprised that the reports on the film cabled by the B.B.C experts, which awaited me at Lobatsi, were most discouraging: I was to find later that with a few notable exceptions everyone in the B.B.C. was exceedingly gloomy about the film's prospects. No producer would appear keen to take on me and my film. I should need all I had of faith, determination, and resource to bring the film undertaking to its desired end. Yet, problematical as it all looked that day in Mafeking, I was lighter at heart after the interview than before it. One reason, I am sure, was that I had kept my promise to Dabé, whom I had left only a few hours before and who was probably still standing at the gate in a fever of waiting for his train to come.

9 The Black-out

Up to that moment I had not really given a thought to the fact that I was now back in my native country. My mind was still deep in a desert world of its own. Moreover, frontiers in Africa are so arbitrarily drawn, so abstract almost, that it is extremely easy to cross them without noticing; but soon after leaving the 'Imperial Reserve', as the people in Mafeking call the enclave on the outskirts of the town where the Bechuanaland administration have their offices and occupy a highly compromising extra-territorial position, I was roughly reminded I had crossed a border in the hearts of men as well as on a map, and was truly home again.

I was driving past a school when I saw a group of small boys dancing in a circle and screaming with excitement. They all wore hats with their school colours on and were striped like little Zebras in blazers of a garish design. On the badges over the breast pockets of the blazers they displayed Baden-Powell's proud motto: 'Never Surrender.' In an open space within the circle another boy, much bigger than the spectators, hatless, face flushed, and tense, was plunging around and hitting, I presumed, another, smaller boy, although I could not be sure because he was invisible behind the dense ring of onlookers. At the corner of the school building behind the boys an elderly coloured man in rags, leaning on a stick, stood with averted face on which there was an expression of acute hopelessness and shame.

It all looked most strange and made me very uneasy. Yet I might have driven straight on if the bigger boy had not stumbled against the spectators and broken through them into the open. He had a thin, undersized coloured boy clasped by the neck tight against his shoulder, and was hitting him as hard as he could in the face with his right fist. The little boy made no effort to fight back: his eyes shut, making no sound, he allowed himself to be pummelled and dragged limp over the ground by the bigger one, while his schoolmates yelled in Afrikaans: 'That's the stuff Apie, *moker** him; *moker* him.' They were all very young, but the yells and the expression on their faces were such as one seldom encounters nowadays except in the demented.

I had beside me in my Land-Rover a stick of good Kalahari wood. Seizing it and braking at the same time, I leapt out of the vehicle. I do not remember precisely what I shouted in Afrikaans at the mob of boys, but I made my meaning plain by going for them and belabouring every shoulder and behind within reach. The mob panicked and fled into the school buildings behind them, the bully at the head of the stampede. Soon I was alone with a little boy lying face down on the ground, too shaken for tears but shivering despite the midsummer heat. The elderly man, coming diffidently towards me, said several times: 'Thank you, my *baas*,† thank you.'

'But what was it all about?' I asked, as we picked up the little boy and put him in the Land-Rover.

He looked at me as if astonished that anyone should think such an occurrence needed a reason, then shook his head, saying like one accustomed to being the accused in court: 'So help me God; I don't know, *baas*. We were just walking by, *baas*, when a little *baas* jumped out, took my grandson by the arm, swore at him and then began beating him. That was all, *baas*, so help me God.'

I talked to him at some length as I took them to their home, and it was clear to me they had given the schoolboys no provocation of any kind. The assault on the little coloured boy was caused not by anything he and his grandfather had done but just by what they were. I longed to account for the incident as the South African version of the sort of bullying that occurs occasionally at the best of schools; but at what other school in the world would bullying receive such enthusiastic applause?

As an indication of the violence gathered just beneath the surface of life in South Africa the incident loomed larger now in my own mind than I would have thought possible. Most of my life I have been conscious of this dark potential in the future of my native country, but never more acutely than now on my return from the desert. It was most odd. I would have said my mind was too deeply preoccupied for so sharp a reaction, but this was not so. At any rate, after the incident at the school I could not separate the

* Apie is an endearment for Abraham and *moker* is a coarse Afrikaans word for a beating up.
† Master.

process which had exterminated the Bushman from the one which set white and black at one another's throats. The Bushman may have vanished from the land, but the war against him goes on as it were by proxy. With the ironic logic of fate the black man, who also destroyed him so ruthlessly, has now inherited his role, being the oldest living exponent of the natural life and the closest equivalent to the Bushman left on the scene.

Wherever I went the sense of conflict grew, the feeling of loss sharpened. What made this more poignant was that a beautiful country had never looked more lovely. The rains had broken in good time and in abundance. As I climbed out of the Kalahari depression on to the high veld, the earth suddenly was summer-young, early awake and quick in silk. The sky was washed clear of dust and the views immense. It was nothing to see the blue-pencil shadow of a rock, forty miles away, draw a precise triangle on a sheet of shining grass, or the volcanic smoke of a storm two days before it broke. Earth and sky, sun and cloud, wind and rain all seemed joined in an overwhelming act of union. With such natural devotion about, the conflict in men confronted one like a desecration of communion. Whenever I thought of the Bushman as I had found him in the Kalahari, the green-gold plains of the high veld, the lone blue koppies of the Free State and Karoo, and the purple mountains of the Cape looked cruelly bereaved and abandoned like great houses wherein the last of a long and devoted line of the men who built them had been murdered. Worst of all, obvious as it was to me, so few of my countrymen seemed aware of how our cruel past had impoverished our present, or appeared apprehensive about the present, let alone the future.

It was extraordinary how most people took for granted the terrible tensions in their lives and the violence gathering in and about them. They seemed to find it perfectly normal to sleep with loaded pistols under their pillows in Johannesburg, to have their houses elaborately wired with electric alarms to the nearest police stations, to have night watchmen armed with clubs patrolling their grounds until morning, and from fear of the blacks to go by closed car for dinner at night to a friend's house barely a hundred yards away. I felt safer alone with my African bush, or with the Bushmen in the heart of the desert, than I did by day in the main streets of the greatest city in South Africa. Nor did the average person appear conscious of the damage inflicted by the national attitude to black and coloured – how it must shatter his own honour and integrity as an individual human being. They behaved as if there were no risks out of the ordinary and they could keep up their negative attitude indefinitely.

It is true they hardly talked any more about anything except their national problems. They had become one of the most subjective peoples on earth. It was alarming how objective lines of communication between them and the world without had broken down. Within a few minutes of greeting one, even old friends seemed incapable of more than a perfunctory inquiry after one's well-being, so eager were they to discuss their public affairs. An elder statesman whom I had known since childhood, for instance, was sitting in the same chair at the same table where I had said good-bye to him five years before. He did not pause to ask me how I was, but beckoned to me urgently to sit beside him and forthwith put to me the same question he had put the last time I saw him. 'What do you think of our native policy now?' There might have been no years between the two occasions, and in a sense there were none: like the rest of the country he was still living in the same moment, only more so.

That is the hallmark of the obsessed: time, losing its true meaning as a process of fulfilment, stands still for them. They are locked out of the healing procession of the seasons. When he had discussed or rather talked at me about his ideas of native policy, this statesman discussed other tensions. They were not hard to come by. South Africa has a greater variety of human tensions than any other country in the world: there are tensions between white and Asians, black and Asians, white and Cape coloureds, Afrikaner and British, and between both Afrikaner and British and black. But he discussed them all entirely as events in a broad external social pattern. There was no hint that he thought the origin of these tensions might also be in himself, or that despite the diversity of the surface patterns they were all members of a single family. Such was the blackout within himself and most of our countrymen.

On my way, I talked about it to one of the Judges of the Supreme Court of Appeal. He is a man who behaved with great courage and integrity during the battle fought in the Law Courts over the removal from the South African Constitution of the entrenched clause which guaranteed the franchise of the Cape coloured people. I told him that what appeared particularly sinister to me was that psychologically we did not see the black and coloured people in Africa at all. I said that vision was complete only if we saw reality with both the outer and the inner eye. Not doing so, we commit the error of the one-eyed vision of which Blake accused the scientist. Our trouble was that we saw the African only with the outer eye and not through the eye of the heart as well. I believed one did not know human beings really until one saw them that way as well – in other words, knew them also through a kind of wonder they provoked in one. Not knowing the African that way, was what I meant by being psychologically blind to him.

He thought about this for a moment before saying, with a note of humility that touched me deeply, that the remark had suddenly taught him something about himself. He said that every day at the end of hours of concentration on the bench he found relaxation in playing a childlike game with himself. He would walk back home from the Supreme Court, pretending he was a kind of Sherlock Holmes and deducing from the appearance of passers-by what their occupations were. For instance, he would say, that young girl judging by her dress must be a typist, that boy an apprentice, that woman a midwife, and the fellow behind her obviously a solicitor. Until I made my remark about our one-eyed vision, he had never realized that he had not yet played the same game with a black or coloured person, though of course there were far more of them about than white people.

Grateful for his response, I told him of something relevant that happened to me once in Switzerland at a conference of Western European writers with writers from behind the Iron Curtain. Someone there one evening in a casual moment spoke with great scorn of Rider Haggard. I had to protest, because modern literature in Africa really began with Rider Haggard. The intellectuals, particularly the French, were horrified by the protest; but the truth is that for us in Africa Rider Haggard was a great pioneer precisely because he played the kind of game with the African which the judge could not play. He was the first to take the African into the fellowship of the imagination. Others had seen the African as an object of pity or derision, a subject for conversion to Christianity, a social problem, a source of labour, a pawn in the class struggle, and new material for social reform. They had projected into him all their own subjective presumptions; but in Rider

Haggard he is admitted to our home of many mansions, a legitimate tenant at last of the human imagination. We could hardly over-estimate the service thus rendered to the future, because this way of knowing not only the African but human beings was what the bleak, impersonal, statistical, and number-mad world of ours had to return to if it were not to dissolve in disaster. Until we considered man, on his journey from the cradle to the grave, with the sort of feelings evoked in us by the sight of a star shooting out of the dark into the dark, we knew him – and ourselves – only in the briefest and least of all his parts. It might sound vague to my friend; but to me it was clear and of the most urgent practical importance to turn back to what we had left of the capacity for wonder; only reverence for life could deliver us from our inhumanity in Africa, and from the cataclysm of violence awaiting us at the end of our present road.

But this sense of wonder, the judge asked sadly – if one has lost it, how does one get it back again? I said I thought he had already shown me how only a few minutes before: by having the humility to recognize what was lacking in the game he played with himself at the end of the day. It might seem nothing to him, but to me it was the germination of a mustard seed, of something that could move mountains. Recognition of what it lacks is one of the most dynamic forces in the human spirit. Realization of our greater selves comes first through the recognition of what we are not. That, I suggested, is the significance in the Sermon on the Mount of the enigmatic 'blessed are the poor in spirit': only the spirit that recognizes itself to be poor, through what it is not, has any promise of increase. We are beggars always to what we were meant to be. It is the failure to recognize this that bars the way and crucifies the new man in us. That was the meaning of the cry: 'Father, forgive them, for they know not what they do.' We are a people, indeed an age, in a dark cloud of unknowing of this kind.

What particularly prevents us from knowing is that the world appears to have lost the sense of the importance of the small in life. Obsessed with mere size and number, we have been deprived of the feeling for the immense significance of the tiny, tentative first movements in the individual heart and imagination. Although our neglect of these impulses is destroying one system after the other around us, we go on ardently giving our allegiance to the great established order, as if its continuance were assured. One look at the identical towns we are building all over the world ought to be enough to show us that this kind of progress is like the proliferation of a single cell at the expense of the rest, which produces the cancer that kills the whole body.

Again, where will we find a government in the modern world, or even a committee, however select, capable of dealing with events in their beginnings? I would say, for instance, that the gravest threat to democracy is precisely the incapacity to deal with incipient events: this is unfortunate, because at its point of origin the gravest event has a certain plastic quality which makes it relatively amenable. Soon, however, events acquire through neglect a twisted character and a vengeful will of their own, as if they have discovered that the world will take them seriously only when they become considerable pressures. So they become explosive. In my own short life in Europe, the Far East, and Africa, I had seen some wonderful, innocent possibilities abandoned on the doorstep of life and allowed to grow into ugly, delinquent children of history, through our sheer inability to perceive their existence, let alone their significance, at the beginning. The point has long been passed where the answer could be found collectively. Today there is no answer and no safety in numbers, only a deadly proliferation of the same peril. The answer must be sought first by the individual alone, as it were in the desert of each of us. We have to accept this sense of something missing, however improbable or insignificant it may seem, as our guide towards distant life-giving waters.

10 Love, the Aboriginal Tracker

Thinking of all this afterwards, I recalled something written many years ago: 'Love is the aboriginal tracker, the Bushman on the faded desert spoor of our lost selves.' There was a great lost world to be rediscovered and rebuilt, not in the Kalahari but in the waste-land of our spirit where we had driven the first things of life, as we had driven the little Bushman into the desert of southern Africa. There was indeed a cruelly denied and neglected first child of life, a Bushman in each of us. I remembered how audiences all over the world reacted when I spoke about the Bushman. Without exception their imaginations were, at the first description of his person, immediately alert. They were audiences of such different histories, cultures, and races as Spanish, Swiss, Italian, Indian, French, Japanese, Finnish, German, Scandinavian, Americans, and assorted British. I felt the Bushman could not have excited the interest of them all unless he represented some elemental common denominator in such diversity of spirit. Most significant, perhaps, was the large number of people who wrote to me saying that they had dreamt about the Bushman after first hearing me talk about him. Many letters would begin in the same way: 'I must tell you: it is so strange. I hardly ever dream, but the night after your talk I had a dream about a Bushman.'

One dream moved me so much that I have remembered it in some detail. It was that of a Spaniard, who told me:

I have not had a dream for years, but last night after the talk I dreamt I was in a great dilapidated building rather like a neglected castle I once knew. Somewhere inside it a woman was weeping as if her heart would break. I rushed from room to room along corridor after corridor and down stair after stair, trying to find her so that I could comfort her. Everywhere I went was empty: the dust thick on the floor and cobwebs on the wall. I was in despair of ever finding her, though the sound of her weeping grew louder and more pitiful in my ears. Suddenly one of your little Bushmen appeared in a window. He beckoned to me urgently

A hammer-head stork

with his bow, indicating that he would lead me to the woman. I started out to follow him, but immediately there was a growl behind me. To my horror one of the fiercest of the wolfhounds, which I let loose in the grounds of my own house as watchdogs every night, leapt forward and dashed straight at the Bushman. I tried to call the hound back but I could not find my voice. In the struggle to find it, I woke up in great distress and could not sleep again. In fact I have felt out of sorts with myself the whole of today. Now what do you say to that?

What indeed could one say about it, even now, except that although these great plains and mountains of South Africa through which I travelled on my way to the sea may know the Bushman no more, 'the prophetic soul of the wide world dreaming on things to come', as Shakespeare put it, knew him still and was glad to meet him again on the lips of living men? Anything that set a dreamless heart dreaming again was not to be despised. For the dream is the keeper of the wonder of which I have spoken. It is there that we must go to 'take upon ourselves the mystery of things as if we were God's spies'. The first time I came across this great cry which would deliver Lear from imprisonment in his own anguish, not by removing his suffering, but by giving it a meaning, the word spies troubled me greatly. After the trumpet call of the opening phrase it sounded oddly perjurative to me. Now I realized it could not have been more apt. Intimation of the new meaning to be lived never comes by battalions but in single spies. It comes as an improbable summons in some lonely, seemingly ill-equipped, and often suffering individual heart, operating far ahead of the armies of new life, like a spy behind the lines of the totalitarian spirit of its day. The mystery we must take upon ourselves in order to free our arrested being is that of the first things of life, which our twentieth-century civilization puts last, but of which the Bushman gives us so consummate an image, representing the child whom we are commanded to humble ourselves before and to become like if we are to enter the Kingdom.

I thought, therefore, I would begin by trying to serve the first things in myself, to turn to the point of origin in myself, to my own moment of innocence when the first things of Africa came over the rim of imagination like starlight out of the night so dearly loved by my native continent. I realized that earliest and latest, old and new, primitive and civilized had met in my life in a way which was perhaps unique. I had experienced primitive Africa, the first life of the land. If I succeeded in rediscovering my own first experience of the first things of Africa, if I honoured them in myself, I might help others to rediscover and honour the same things in themselves. It would not matter that I possessed no expert training or special knowledge. Consciously or unconsciously, one lives not only one's own life but also the life of one's time. What was valid in my own experience would be valid in a measure also for my own day. I could let my experience of the primitive pattern of creation speak for me, since I have taken part in the most ancient working of the human spirit as it had been transmitted from the lives of the first people of Africa. I would merely be the bridge between the first pattern of things and my own time. I would use what knowledge I had of the first Africa, in particular the little I had now learnt of the Bushman, his mind and way of life in the desert, merely to interpret the experience into a contemporary idiom and so try to make it accessible to the modern imagination. That, however amateurish or small, could be the beginning of better things, because what the world lacks today is not so much knowledge of these first things as experience of them.

We know so much intellectually, indeed, that we are in danger of becoming the prisoners of our knowledge. We suffer from a hubris of the mind. We have abolished superstition of the heart only to install a superstition of the intellect in its place. We behave as if there were some magic in mere thought, and we use thinking for purposes for which it was never designed. As a result we are no longer sufficiently aware of the importance of what we cannot know intellectually, what we must know in other ways, of the living experience before and beyond our transitory knowledge. The passion of the spirit, which would inspire man to live his finest hour dangerously on the exposed frontier of his knowledge, seemed to me to have declined into a vague and arid restlessness hiding behind an arrogant intellectualism, like a child of arrested development behind the skirts of its mother.

Intellectually, modern man knows almost all there is to know about the pattern of creation in himself, the forms it takes, the surface designs it describes. He has measured the pitch of its rhythms and carefully recorded all the mechanics. From the outside he sees the desirable first object of life more clearly perhaps than man has ever seen it before. But less and less does he experience the process within. Less and less is he capable of committing himself body and soul to the creative experiment that is continually seeking to fire him and to charge his little life with great objective meaning. Cut off by accumulated knowledge from the heart of his own living experience, he moves among a comfortable rubble of material possession, alone and unbelonging, sick, poor, starved of meaning. How different the naked little Bushman, who could carry all he possessed in one hand. Whatever his life lacked, I never felt it was meaning. Meaning for him died only when we bent him to our bright twentieth-century will. Otherwise, he was rich where we were poor; he walked clear-cut through my mind, clothed in his own vivid experience of the dream of life within him. By comparison most of the people I saw on my way to the sea were blurred, and like the knight at arms in Keats' frightening allegory, 'palely loitering' through life.

The essence of all this was put to me once by a great hunter, who was born in Africa, and who died there after having wandered all over it for seventy years, from the trembling Bushveld of the Transvaal to where the baroque mountains of Abyssinia dwindle down in dead hills to the Red Sea. Africa, he told me, was truly God's country – the last in the world perhaps with a soul of its own; and the difference between those born of its great earth and those who invaded it from Europe and Asia was simply the difference between *being* and *having*. He said the natural child of Africa *is*; the European or Asian *has*. He was not alone in this assessment of the conflict: the primitive keepers of the soul of Africa were keenly aware of its dangers to the being of man. I could give many instances of this awareness manifesting itself tragically in the history of Africa, from the time my ancestors landed at the Cape of Good Hope three hundred years ago, to Mau Mau in Kenya and the latest series of ritual murders; but I prefer to give an illustration from my own life.

Soon after leaving school I heard that a new prophet had arisen among the great Zulu nation of South Africa. I was greatly excited by the news. Africa was still profoundly an Old Testament country, and the appearance of a prophet seemed not only natural and right but also an event that might be of some cosmic importance. I went to see him as soon as I could. He lived in a round kraal of grass beehive huts on a hill standing among the complex of chasms and gorges of a deep and intricate valley in Natal. It was early summer – one of those days that come over the edge of time charged with a meaning of their own. The valley was overflowing with light, sensitive and trembling like a heart with its first apprehension of love. On the slope of the hill a long line of women were hoeing the magenta earth. They were naked to the waist; their strong bodies and full breasts were aubergine coloured in the sun. As they worked they sang altogether in soft voices a song of the earth, whose rhythm was so in accord with the pulse of the light and the water-wheel-turn of the day in the blue sky that it made one great round of summer music. From the slopes beyond came the clear bright voices of the young boys herding the cattle and talking easily to one another, often a mile apart. Sometimes, too, one heard a cow calling for her calf, a goat's bright bleat or a donkey's shattering plea for compassion, but the sound of the singing set to the rhythm of the day dominated the valley.

The first indication I had that the prophet was coming to meet us was when the singing stopped abruptly. The women ceased hoeing and turned to look down the hill behind them. From the bed of the stream below, a man emerged. He was tall, dressed in a white gown that fell to his feet, and with a long staff in his hand he slowly climbed the hill towards us, as if deep in thought. The women watched him with such close attention that one felt every step he took was fateful. At one moment I thought the women were going to break off working altogether and form up in a body behind him to escort him back to his kraal: but he made a gesture with his long arm, dignified and imperative, which immediately set them to work again, hoeing with such a will that the dust flickered like fire around their feet. Noticing this my guide, a Zulu chief himself, smiled with a dark satisfaction and remarked: 'Not by the men, but by the women who flock to him and their obedience, shall you first know the true prophet.'

When the seer stood before us at last, raising his hand palm-outwards in the ancient Zulu greeting, I thought I had never seen a more beautiful person. His head was round and shapely, his forehead broad, his features sensitive, the face as a whole naturally ascetic without being either austere or fanatic. His eyes were big and well-spaced, having the look of a personality in whom nothing was hidden. His hands were those of an artist, and he used them delicately to point his words. On his head he wore the round ring which among his people is a sign that the man is complete. He wore his ring so naturally that it did not seem to be imposed from without, but rather to emanate from him like a halo from a saint.

Outside his kraal there was a large wild fig tree whose dark green leaves were wet with light. We sat down in its shade and talked until the sun went down red behind the blue rim of the valley filled with evening smoke. The more we talked, the more I felt that I was not in the twentieth century but some early Biblical hour. We talked about a great many things of immense interest – I shall refer to them later – yet about the subject that mattered most to me I was disappointed. When I begged him to speak of the first spirit of the Zulu nation, Umkulunkulu, the Great One, he shook his beautiful old head and said with infinite sadness: 'We do not speak of Umkulunkulu any longer. His praise-names are forgotten. People now talk only of things that are useful to them.'

Recalling this conversation, which took place nearly thirty-five years ago, I realized that the situation which I believe we are all facing in the world today was one which the primitive world, the past life of Africa, knew only too well. It is a loss of first spirit, or to put it in the old-fashioned way, a loss of soul. Before my day with the Zulu prophet was over, I knew that he regarded this as the greatest calamity that could come to human beings. Other examples flooded my mind of how the keepers of man's first spirit in Africa constantly warned him against this peril. Indeed, the primitive world regarded the preservation of first spirit as the greatest, most urgent of all its tasks. It designed elaborate ritual, ceaselessly fashioned myths, legends, stories, and music, to contain the meaning and feed the fire of the creative soul.

Here, from far back in my childhood, the memory of one of the servants in our large patriarchal household joined that of the Zulu seer. She was the lowest in the long hierarchy of black and coloured servants; yet, when we were hurt or distressed, she was the one we used to go to for comfort. One cold winter's evening when I could not sleep, she told me this story.

There was once, she said, a man of the early race who possessed a wonderful herd of cattle: every beast in the herd matched the others in coats of black and white stipples. She stressed the colour of the cattle repeatedly. Even then, young as I was, I had an idea how important the matter of colour was. Cattle were never mere cattle to primitive men, but creatures full of rare and ancient spirit. As he listened to them lowing in his kraal after the lion's roar or the leopard's cough, he heard again the accents of his ancestors. When they were born he regarded the colour of their coats closely because it showed some meaning, some degree of favour or disfavour on the part of the great spirit over all. He had single adjectives for describing each combination of colour, and was never compelled to use a phrase like 'a sort of strawberry roan' to designate an animal: there was one exact word to do it for him. As a child I knew eight such adjectives for which we had no single equivalent in any European tongue.

This combination of black and white in cattle was the greatest and most significant colour scheme of all, and the word for it had profound mystical associations. For instance, I was once with our black herdsmen when a cow was safely delivered of a black and white stippled calf: the cry of joy, reverence, and gratitude to creation for so great a favour, which broke from their deep throats was one of the most wonderful sounds I have ever heard. I knew too a tribe who, when a man among them died, brought the finest white and black stippled cow in his possession to the side of the open grave. There they made it lower its head so that it could look its dead master in the face for the last time. Thereafter it belonged utterly to the spirits, and no one in the dead man's family would ever dream of killing or selling it.

There was meaning in everything for the first people – from the birth of a calf to the death of a man and beyond; and enclosing all, there was an overwhelming sense that every living thing shared in the process of creation. When our servant told me how this man of the early race possessed cattle with such numenous hides, my child's imagination anticipated a story of more than usual significance, and I could not keep still in bed for excitement.

This man of the early race, therefore, she told me, dearly loved his black and white cattle. He always took them out into the veld himself, chose the best possible grazing for them, and watched over them like a mother over her children, seeing that no wild animals came near to hurt or disturb them. In the evening he would bring them back to his kraal, seal the entrance carefully with branches of the toughest thorn, and, watching them contentedly chewing the cud, think, 'In the morning I shall have a wonderful lot of milk to draw from them.' One morning, however, when he went to his kraal expecting to find the udders of the cows full and sleek with milk, he was amazed to see they were slack, wrinkled and empty. He thought with immediate self-reproach he had chosen their grazing badly, and took them to better grass. He brought them home in the evening and again thought, 'Tomorrow for a certainty I shall get more milk than ever before'; but again in the morning the udders were slack and dry. For the second time he changed their grazing, and yet again the cows had no milk. Disturbed and suspicious, he decided to keep a watch on the cattle throughout the dark.

In the middle of the night he was astonished to see a cord of finely-woven fibre descending from the stars; and down this cord, hand over hand, one after another came some young women of the people of the sky. He saw them, beautiful and gay, whispering and laughing softly among themselves, steal into the kraal and milk his cattle dry with calabashes. Indignant, he jumped out to catch them but they scattered cleverly so that he did not know which way to run. In the end he did manage to catch one; but while he was chasing her the rest, calabashes and all, fled up the sky, withdrawing the cord after the last of them so that he could not follow. However, he was content because the young woman he had caught was the loveliest of them all. He made her his wife and from that moment he had no more trouble from the people of the sky.

His new wife now went daily to work in the fields for him while he tended his cattle. They were happy and they prospered. There was only one thing that worried him. When he caught his wife she had a basket with her. It was skilfully woven, so tight that he could not see through it, and was always closed firmly on top with a lid that fitted exactly into the opening. Before she would marry him, his wife had made him promise that he would never lift the lid of the basket and look inside until she gave him permission to do so. If he did a great disaster might overtake them both. But as the months went by, the man began to forget his promise. He became steadily more curious, seeing the basket so near day after day, with the lid always firmly shut. One day when he was alone he went into his wife's hut, saw the basket standing there in the shadows, and could bear it no longer. Snatching off the lid, he looked inside. For a moment he stood there unbelieving, then burst out laughing.

When his wife came back in the evening she knew at once what had happened. She put her hand to her heart, and looking at him with tears in her eyes, she said: 'You've looked in the basket.'

He admitted it with a laugh, saying: 'You silly woman. You silly, silly creature. Why have you made such a fuss about this basket? There's nothing in it at all.'

'Nothing?' she said, hardly finding the strength to speak.

'Yes, nothing,' he answered emphatically.

At that she turned her back on him, walked away straight into the sunset and vanished. She was never seen on earth again.

To this day I can hear the old black servant woman saying to me: 'And do you know why she went away, my little master? Not because he had broken his promise but because, looking into the basket, he had found it empty. She went because the basket was not empty: it was full of beautiful things of the sky she stored there for them both, and because he could not see them and just laughed, there was no use for her on earth any more and she vanished.'

That story seems to me an accurate image of our predicament in the world now, both as individuals and as nations. The primitive spirit stands in rags and tatters, rejected by the contemporary mind, offering us such warnings. Laughing, unaware of peril, we lift the lids of our own particular baskets and, blindly declaring them to be empty, we lose our soul, of which woman is the immemorial image.

It is true there is no resolution, only tragedy and a warning, in this African tale. But the woman who walked into the blood-red sunset of Africa to vanish, the servants in rags and tatters still haunting the corridors of my own mind, the woman abandoned and weeping in the ruined castle in the dream of the Spaniard, and indeed the naked, demented Bushman woman whimpering in the summer sunlight of the desert, each in her own way seemed to serve a single meaning. They all drew attention to the denial of something vital in the human spirit. The denial might be caused as in the African tale by the unawareness of man, whose vision is so tied to the world *without* that he is incapable of seeing the spiritual content of his own inner world. It might be caused by the cruelty of man, who trespasses against his own humanity in doing violence to earth's children; or by mere inability to control that fierce watchdog of our daylight selves – the mind narrowed to an aggressive materialistic rationalism, as in the dream of the Spaniard who could not call back the wolfhound he kept to guard his home and treasured possessions.

The general state of neglect can be symbolized by a ruined castle, a desert in southern Africa, or a despised basket in the shadows of an African hut. But they all conveyed only one thing to me – the peril of man when divorced from the first things in himself. Cut off from them for long, he loses his meaning just as that man of the early race, blind to the contents of the basket, lost his lovely lady of the starry sky; and only those who have seen the stars of Africa can know how terrible such a loss must have been. This peril appeared so active in the world around me that I felt I could say of it, as Dabé said of the Bushman woman at Gemsbok Pan, 'The time of the hyena is upon us.'

However, once I had discovered the kinship of these images, so far apart in their origins yet so closely related in their meaning. I began to consider more carefully the rest of the pattern of the first things of Africa. In particular, I examined the pattern of the Bushman as experienced through my own life and imagination. It was so much older than even the earliest known pattern of the most primitive of black races in Africa. It was, as far as I knew, the purest manifestation of life lived in the beginning according to life's own design rather than man's wilful and one-sided plan for it. It is true, I was not without prejudice in the matter, for I had a private hope of the utmost importance to me. The Bushman's physical shape combined those of a child and a man: I surmised that examination of his inner life might reveal a pattern which reconciled the spiritual opposites in the human being and made him whole.

More immediately, his tragedy was the only one I knew of in Africa for which white and black shared an equal guilt. In the long and terrible history of Africa it was the one mirror wherein both white and black could clearly view not the unreal and conflicting abstractions they have made of one another, but what is so tragically hidden from them – their common, fallible, and bewildered human faces. If that could be done, it might start the first movement towards a reconciliation, first in their imagination and then in their lives. But apart from these private rationalizations, I was compelled towards the Bushman like someone who walks in his sleep, obedient to a dream of finding in the dark what the day has denied him.

So I collected all I could discover of what has been written about the Bushman. I had read it all many times before in my life. It had become part of my imaginative experience: but, knowing how different just one of the Bushman legends had appeared to me after my journey into the desert, I was determined to take nothing for granted. I would pool all I had learnt in the past with what I had brought back with me from the desert, and see what came out of it at leisure on the long voyage back to England by sea. I boarded my ship in Table Bay, more tired than I had been for years because of the long and almost disastrous journey behind me, yet inwardly refreshed and strangely excited. I thought it a good omen that on the desk in my cabin I found two telegrams from Gobabis on the far western fringe of the desert. One read: 'Your Bushman arrived safely by train ex-Windhoek today.' The other informed me:'As per instructions one Bushman consigned Gemsbok Pan-wards by Government lorry two a.m. today stop detailed account expenses follows.'

Part Three: World Regained

There is a dream dreaming us.

BUSHMAN HUNTER TO WRITER

11 Dxui – Creation and Re-creation

In the beginning, St John says, was the Word. I believe that is a way of saying that in the beginning there was meaning. This word, this meaning, according to the Bible was with God and indeed was God. The ancient Chinese said something similar when they defined meaning as that which has always existed through itself. Somehow this meaning demanded also to be lived. As St John puts it again, the word was made flesh. A similar intimation of its beginnings seems to me present in the first spirit of Africa. It is true the Bushmen I had just met in the Kalahari were not very communicative in this respect. I think it needed more time, more trust and patience than I commanded to elicit from them the full image in which this intimation moves over the mystery of the beginning in their spirit in search of some conscious thought to contain it, like the first bird let out of the ark winging over the dark waters of the Old Testament flood for some tangible fact of earth or rock to light upon. When I pressed them to talk to me about the beginning they seemed to lose their power of speech, and the only significant answer was given to me one night by my favourite hunter. Distressed by my persistence and his inability to satisfy my curiosity, he said: 'But you see, it is very difficult, for always there is a dream dreaming us.'

It was a pregnant hint. Quite apart from its likeness to the Shakespearian assertion, 'We are such stuff as dreams are made on', it confirmed the observation of the Frenchman, who was among the first to examine the life of primitive people with no feeling of superiority or abhorrence, that 'the dream is the true God of primitive man'. Believing as I do that the dream is not a waste product of the mind expelled through some sewage system of the spirit but a manifestation of first and abiding meaning, I thought I should enlarge St John's theme to include the idea that in the beginning there was a dream. This dream was with God and indeed was God. Somehow this dream demanded that it should be lived.

As St John might have put it, 'the dream was made flesh'.

Fortunately I did not have just this one statement of a contemporary stone-age hunter to go by. In the few myths, legends, and stories left us, a dream contains the heart of the matter. All this will emerge, I hope from the natural progression of the key stories towards greater awareness in the mind of the first people of Africa; but here I remember in particular a more specific and elaborate presentation of the first spirit of creation. It was obtained by Bleek* nearly eighty years ago from two little Bushman boys who came from the same desert world as my hunter. Young as they were, they had already been instructed in the first spirit of creation and spoke of it in a manner which bears comparison with almost any imaginative representation of the beginning of things. They called the first spirit of creation, to use Bleek's spelling, Dxui. How I long to have been there to hear its electricity on their lips. On my own, carefully following Bleek's system and guided by what I know of Bushman sound, it brings echoes of the explosion in thought with which the image of God first burst through the sound-barriers of the human mind to acquire a definite name. Throughout the Bushman children's statement this name and this sound are constantly reiterated with the assertion: 'And Dxui was Dxui.' God was God and the meaning was meaning.

'His works are many,' one little Bushman told Bleek. 'And were not one but many, and my father's father told me of his doings, for his works are numerous.' When the sun rose, he went on, Dxui was a flower. The birds ate of him as a flower until the sun set. The night fell. He lay down and slept. The place was dark and the sun rose. Dxui, tall as a tree, was another and larger kind of flower, but when the night fell Dxui was Dxui. The sun rose and Dxui again was a flower – a light-coloured flower that turned into a green fruit which ripened red in time, but when the sun went down again Dxui was a man and rested. When the sun rose again, Dxui was Dxui and went away to become a palm; and at sunset he was again a man: but when the sun rose (as if flesh and blood were still more than he could bear) he was once more a species of plant of which there are many kinds and a great abundance from shrubs to trees, all bearing fruit of red and gold. The sun set again and he was just he and lay upon the ground and slept.

But now a new note breaks in. The dread word which seems to

* See Introduction.

precede the vital act of all conscious creation is uttered: he was alone. He had, of course, been alone before, because in the beginning he was just he; but for the first time now he is aware of being alone, he has been overtaken at last by this sense I have mentioned before, of being a single spy, the mystery of first things full upon him. When the sun rose and he awoke out of his aloneness and stood up, he saw the sun. It was, the Bushman children said, only a little sun – the Bushman way of saying that the sun was no longer adequate, the shadow of Dxui's aloneness had diminished its light. So he became a new kind of tree – a tree with a difference, since although it bore fruit, it was also covered with thorns – the first emblem of worldly rejection and inner loneliness. At this moment inevitably his woman appears. She sees Dxui as the tree, goes at once to take some of its fruit, but the tree vanishes. One longs to have been there to ask the little Bushman children why, but this is the first lesson to be grasped: beginning is nothing if not axiomatic; it neither allows nor needs any proof or any explanation; it can only be accepted for its intrinsic truth. There is no *why* in the beginning, only a *thus*. If we are faithful to the *thus*, we may arrive at some glimmering of the *why*.

The woman wanted to possess the fruit of the tree, and as a result the tree vanished and Dxui became a creature of wings. He was a fly. As a fly he humbly settled on the grass, and presumably was alone again. This was tragedy for them both. Clearly they had a profound need of each other, for the woman lay down upon the earth and cried about the tree of fruit that had vanished, and crying she died. In other words, an essential aspect of the first meaning of things, which the woman personifies, had as yet been denied life.

Then Dxui became water. Again and again in the unfolding of the archetypal pattern, when the new, larger life is threatened or denied, when death and disaster seem to have ended the search of the spirit for greater meaning, we find this image of water, and through water a certainty of renewal. It is so in the Old Testament; it is so in parable and baptism in the New; it recurs throughout the story of the first spirit of Africa. So Dxui was water. It is true he was not large water. The little Bushman said he was only a small water appropriate, I assume, to the image of rebeginning; but this water was blessed with the shadow of a tree whose fruit the wood pigeons came to eat.

Here is the process of unending change and inevitable renewal – the quest of meaning for articulate form and the rejection of the form that is inadequate, the demand badly lived the day before to be newly lived on the day after. Re-reading the little Bushman's account of Dxui, I not only felt a strange emotional parallel with the Genesis of the Bible, but seemed to discern also a prototype of Goethe finding, as he put it, the signature of God in all things, or of the great Flemish poet Guido Gezelle who, watching a water bug on a pond, asked: 'Oh! you twisting and turning water thing, what are you doing there with your small black waistcoat on?' and was answered: 'I write and re-write everlastingly the word of God.'

After water, Dxui becomes another flower, a bird, the snarer of the bird, the eater of the bird. For the first time he is not eaten, but himself eats: he experiences a new hunger for being. After that he takes on fresh stature as a man, and as a result he is soon a man rejected and hunted down by other men. In the moment of rejection he becomes the tears that fall out of the eyes of the Bushman, himself one of the most despised and rejected of men. At this point I felt myself in the presence of one of the great discoveries on the road of the first spirit – the finding of a greater new world than Columbus ever discovered; the place of compassion in the spirit of creation. The anguish of Dxui's discovery made him cry, so the little Bushman children said, rendering one of the most pitiful of the Bushman sounds: 'Ye-he! Ye-he! Ye-he!'

Through this gift of compassion discovered in himself life itself is transformed. Though his enemies use the sound to track him down, his tears grow wings. Dxui becomes a greater bird and goes winging back to the place of his father and mother. Before the next phase of renewal, before returning to the search for greater meaning in the world without, he makes the full circle of his beginnings. A sort of prodigal who has exhausted his rich interlude of creation, he goes home, but it is in a sense a return more meaningful than that of the prodigal son of the Bible, who went back to the home of a father only, for the parable makes no mention of a mother. Dxui, the little Bushman said, goes back 'to the place' of his father and his mother. It is the Bushman way of saying that through his experience of rejection he discovers the two sources of his creative self, the female and the male, mother and father, unconscious and conscious, the feeling and the thought, the love and the authority.

In that return he reassumes his full stature as the Dxui that was always Dxui: he calls out to his father as if in pain, begging for forgiveness, 'My father, oh!' His father instantly responds, 'My child! Oh!' and goes towards him. As the father turns towards him Dxui dies as a man and turns into a lizard. To anyone ignorant of the aboriginal language of the spirit, this may come as sheer bathos. But it is well that one should get used to it as soon as possible. The first spirit of Africa speaks not in words so much as in images. Its images are carefully chosen to convey meaning. What moves me most about it is the complete absence of sentimentality: the fable makes no concession to privilege of mind or prejudice of heart; it is utterly single in its devotion to the service of meaning. To say that Dxui died and became a lizard is the Bushman way of stating that the first spirit of creation is finally and irrevocably committed also to life on earth. The lizard is chosen because there is hardly a living creature closer to the earth. The mole, the worm, and the serpent are more within it; but a lizard is upon it, walking on feet of its own close to the earth, yet living between it and the sky. Besides, the lizard is extremely old – among the very first of living things upon earth.

There then we leave Dxui committed to life on earth, committed to begin again humbly, great spirit that he is – a mere lizard in the dust. The account closes with all sorts of hints about the repercussions of this humble commitment throughout the universe. It is clear that one of the consequences had something to do with the discovery of fire, since Dxui's father is frequently reported as saying that he saw his child making fire, 'rubbing fire, the fire of little sticks' before he died as 'Dxui' and became 'another person'. That aspect I will deal with fully in its natural place, but this much belongs here: all the hints and implications of the story point to a single end: the first spirit of creation is committed to life on earth and a great act of discrimination has taken place in the totality of the spirit. Where there had been a Dxui who was always Dxui, there are now a great father and a great mother as well as a son come to earth.

It is true that, as in so many accounts of the beginning of things all over the world, the great mother vanishes soon: she is not remembered except in a statement by another Bushman to Stow* that the first person of all creation was a woman. Nor is anything

* See Introduction.

more said of the attempt to give life to the other woman, the feminine aspect of Dxui on earth during his moment of aloneness as a tree of thorns under a sun that was 'only a little sun'. This first light of the spirit, this ancient old dawn of Africa, is focused upon the drama of the father and the son in Dxui. They have recognized the difference in their one-ness or, to put it in the ortho-dox Western way, God and His creation have separated from one another. What is described as the first disobedience and the fall of man occurred. Adam the lizard is out of the garden of fruit-bearing plants and trees, and pigeons singing ardently among trembling leaves, where he was at one with his spirit before the coming of the word and the descent of meaning to the earth.

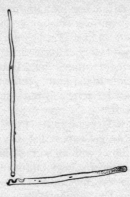

Fire-sticks

We are a long way from the realization that this act of disobedi-ence, this separation is necessary in order to achieve a more mean-ingful obedience, a greater reunion and oneness of life. But another of the tiny, humble, painful movements towards it has been accom-plished and for the moment there is no feeling of achievement, only the immediate sense of the pain and shock of the separation. It may be that the day is just the dream of the night: consciousness may be, as I believe, the deepest and most cherished dream of the un-conscious first spirit of life, yet at this moment in the dawning awareness of my native land, there is only separation and a grow-ing knowledge of the pain of being separate, wringing from Dxui's father the cry of self-reproach, 'And I did not see my child.' With deepening anguish, he explores the nature of his separation from his son, finally saying: 'I go to my country and my country is far away, and many moons I go to my country and do not see my country . . . and my child is another person . . . today I am afraid of my child and go to my own country.' His own country, so the little Bushman children said, was a large mountain. The first spirit of Africa was to have its Sinai too.

12 Dxui and Mantis

It took me some time to realize that in my journey to the desert behind me I had been, if not to the original, then to a facsimile of the mountain of Dxui's father. The story of my journey to the 'Slippery Hills' in the desert and the strange things that befell us there is told in detail in *The Lost World of the Kalahari*. I had read about Dxui years previously, but I cannot recall that the story had made any except a vaguely poetic impression on me. Like almost all the Bushman stories of the past, I did not understand it as I understood it now after a grown-up experience of the Bushman and his ways. I can honestly say I never gave this written account of Dxui a conscious thought and did not even remember his name until I saw it in Bleek's book again. Yet all the time I was at the Slippery Hills I had the feeling that I was in a great and ancient temple. Indeed from the moment I first saw them rising suddenly out of the flat plain after weeks of travelling across the long un-differentiated desert levels, I had the same quickening of the senses and upsurge of emotion that made the psalmist cry out aloud: 'I will lift up mine eyes unto the hills, from whence cometh my help.'

Of course the old African prophet who took me there had done his best to induce an attitude of reverence towards the hills by telling me beforehand that they were sacred and the home of every great and ancient spirit. There was the pool of water that never dried up and beside it the tree with the fruit of knowledge upon it. There too were the marks in the rock where the great spirit had knelt to pray on the day of his first creation. I had seen for myself some of the essential elements of the story of Dxui still held in reverence there by living man. I had now no doubt that the Slippery Hills were once a Bushman temple to the first spirit of creation and that, vague as Bleek's account of Dxui may sound in an age obsessed with concrete, it referred to something so real to the Bushman that they dedicated mountains to it, decorating their rocks with all the love and skill of which their painters were capable. What made me more certain of it than ever was that 'He who was left after reaping', as the prophet was called, belonged to a tribe called Makoba. Eighty years before, the little Bushman children told Bleek that Dxui in his first tentative metamorphosis into man was a Makoba too.

Kalahari rock decorated with eland painting

Much as all this meant to me, it still left a very incomplete picture of the first spirit. Fortunately the theme was much more highly and vigorously developed among the Bushmen who inhabited my own part of South Africa, some of whom for centuries congregated at the three-eyed fountain on my grandfather's farm. Among them the first spirit was not known as Dxui but as Kaggen. Considering the miles and the deserts in between them and the country of Bleek's little children, it would have been surprising if there had not been this and other differences as well. Nevertheless Dxui much resembles the great hero of creation, Kaggen, the praying mantis whom we meet in the imagination of the Bushman of the interior of Africa where I was born. The main difference, perhaps, though one must be careful not to build too much on such fragments, is that of vigour.

Dxui, in the account of the Bushman children, is a tentative, sensitive, introverted spirit, however great and numerous his works. Beside what was to follow, Dxui is almost a sort of Hamlet who shrinks into nothing at the approach of his Ophelia and ends up by losing mother as well as father. Yet to me nothing could seem more right than that at the point of origin the first movement of the spirit of creation should be centrifugal. All beginning is profoundly paradoxical, as if it can only be outward bound through an inward way, so that Dxui satisfies my own imagination as an image of the first manifestation of creation.

Yet I would not be content, were there not also this development of the theme of creation in Kaggen who strides boldly into battle for greater meaning, a complex figure of god and mortal. Yet never does Mantis make me feel that he has replaced or contradicted Dxui; rather he has made him more complete, for the two aspects are of one and the same meaning. The objective evidence for their essential one-ness is not great, but I believe it is conclusive. First of all there is in general a similarity between their roles of creation; Dxui for example is described as carrying over his shoulder the bag of antelope skin which was one of the most important items of Mantis's equipment. Then Dxui is the first of whom it is said that he made fire. One of Mantis's nicknames was 'old maker of fire', or 'old Tinderbox' as the tame Bushman of the Cape called him. Mantis too was the bringer of the word, for he it was, the Bushman said, who first gave things their names. And in the beginning, the word again. Finally there is the fact that Dxui's first metamorphosis was into a flower. To this day the remnants of Bushman left in the country Bleek's young informants came from say that a mantis was carried by a bee over the darkened waters of the flood at the beginning of things. Worn-out and desperate for a place to rest with its heavy load in that formless waste, the bee saw a great white flower, half open above the flood. With its dying energy it laid Mantis to rest in the heart of the flower and placed the seed of the first spirit inside it, safe from the turbulent waters sweeping by without.* That alone would have been proof enough for me, because it fitted in with one of my earliest experiences of the first things in Africa.

My old coloured nurse Klara, who had a Bushman mother and to whom *The Lost World of the Kalahari* is dedicated, showed me my first praying mantis. It is so far back in time that there is almost no surround to the experience. About the first thing I remember in life is the light of a high-veld sunset aflame in the necklace of large glass beads round Klara's yellow throat. Immediately thereafter came the mantis. Only we did not call him Mantis; we called him the Hottentot's God, because that was the name we had inherited from our careless past. Our ancestors, when they landed at the Cape of Good Hope over three hundred years ago, could not tell

* Schoeman, *Hunters of the Desert Land*, Allen & Unwin, 1958.

the Bushman at first from the Hottentot, who is nearest to him both physically and culturally, just as many people still cannot tell the difference between Japanese and Chinese. When they noticed the reverence in which the mantis was held by some of the aborigines of the Cape, they inaccurately called him the Hottentot's God. Actually the Hottentots had a first spirit of their own far higher in the biological scale of evolution than any insect. Mantis was peculiarly the Bushman's figure of the first spirit of creation and should have been called the Bushman's God. But Klara, untroubled by any confusion of names, playing with me one day on the grass, suddenly stopped and exclaimed with a deep note of pleasure I had never heard before: 'Oh! Look. The Hottentot's God.'

There beside us on the grass was a mantis, very still, head turned on one side as if listening to something that we could not hear. I

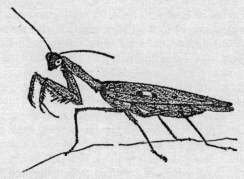

Hottentot's God or praying mantis

held my breath with awe at the sight of this strange silent, oddly contemplative thing that had suddenly appeared out of nowhere in the grass beside us, while Klara's behaviour increased the sense of the miraculous in the occasion.

'Oh look and watch!' she whispered so that I could barely hear. She went down on her knees beside the mantis, bowing to it with her hands folded in front of her like a Christian at prayer. Calling it a name I had not heard and cannot remember, she begged of the mantis in a low hissing voice: 'Please, how low is the sea?' To my amazement the head of the mantis turned and he looked straight

149

before him, while the two long front feet held limp in front of him suddenly moved and pointed downwards to the earth.

'Please, how high is the sea?' Klara asked.

Mantis lifted his head, looked up and raised his long front feet to point at the cloudless blue sky. I could not make sense of the questions or Mantis's positive response to them. Klara had never been to the sea. We were at that moment some thousand miles from the nearest coastline and she was to die, alas, without ever seeing the sea. Yet her attitude of extreme reverence, the strange shape of Mantis, his uncanny responsiveness to the sound of worship on her tongue, and her extreme delight at the outcome made an impression I was never to forget.

The next time I saw a mantis I thought I would try the questions for myself. When it failed to respond, in spite of my doing my utmost to imitate Klara's tone and manner, I tried to push its forefeet in the desired direction with a stem of grass. At that moment it turned its head with a sharp angular movement like a puppet. Its eyes seemed to flash with anger; it gave me such a fierce look that I stopped, suddenly apprehensive, but not before Klara had seen what I was doing, rushed up, smacked the hand that held the stem of grass, and whisked me away.

That night as she put me to bed, remorseful for having been rough with me, she said: 'We never tease the mantis. We never ask anything of the mantis for fun. We never ask unless we ask it here from the heart.' At that she laid her hand on her own warm heart.

For years I wondered at odd moments about Klara's questions to the mantis: 'How high and how low is the sea?' The less I saw a meaning in them, the more I seemed to be convinced of the existence of one. Now with the story of Mantis in the heart of a great half-open white flower braving the flood, I thought I had my code to the cypher wherein the first spirit communicates most immediately with life. These questions were the essential opening preliminaries to a Bushman's prayer, because they recognized Mantis's presence in the beginning when life first rose above the tides that would have overwhelmed it. The sea, the great water as the Bushman called it, was the image in Klara's mind of the flood in the beginning. Because Mantis was there, he could report faithfully on the state of the tide in the spirit.

The longer I lived with this image the more wonderful it became. I never cease to be amazed now at the native integrity of the Bush-

'... *the angry cobra erect*'

man imagination that could choose it and then cling unfailingly to it in the great and bewitching context of Africa. For there has never been another continent with such a variety and abundance of natural life. There are found in it more than a hundred and twenty different kinds of antelope; there are more varieties of cats, from magnetic lions and leopards to starry-eyed lynxes; more snakes, from the angry cobra erect and spitting in the sun to the bold and burnished mamba; more birds, from the ostrich, earth-bound for a Promethean sin, and burning flamingos which set white water on fire, to the tiny tinkling little tin-tinkies; more insects, from the mosquitoes rising to the sound of bagpipe music in the tidal waves of smoke over the marshes, to locusts darkening the day at noon, than on any other land on earth.

From birth to death the Bushman carried this ancient image of

Mantis in a country bursting its seams with natural life. I myself have seen birds come all day long over the horizon like the smoke of a prairie fire; locusts rising over the hills in clouds at dawn, and at sunset still travelling in the same unbroken line of cloud above us. I have walked by vast inland waters which at twilight had no more room for the birds to settle, forcing thousands more to go in search of parking accommodation and to vanish, streaking through the last pink zone of the gathering night. I still see lions in a pride of as much as thirty, elephants in hundreds. Even in the desert just behind me I had seen springbuck in their gold and white, bubbling like foam around me.

What it must have been like at first light in Africa we can only guess; but what we do know is that with all that bewildering richness of choice around him, the Bushman chose the humble mantis. Unlike others among the primitive races of Africa, who confided their sense of the first spirit to splendid and imposing creatures of the land like the elephant, the buffalo, the python, the crocodile, the gorilla, or black-and-white stippled bulls in their kraals, the Bushman chose the physically insignificant, and having done so he stuck to it. He may have had, as children have, so fine a sense of the great in the small and the small in the great because he himself was so small; it was certainly not from any indifferences to the great and brilliant figures in the pageantry of Africa. His paintings on the rocks clearly show how he loved these and shared with them a feeling of participation in the design of creation. His stories show how for him they too trailed clouds of glory from the first spirit that was their common home. They all had a place by such fire as he had in that home; but in the light of that fire Mantis ruled. I believe it was so because the point of meaning in life is naturally Euclidean: it is position in the spirit that matters, not magnitude; and since the Bushman's spirit was enclosed in the first nature of Africa as a fish in the sea, his imagination – like that of Blake, whom I always think of as the great Bushman poet of England – was naturally predisposed to see infinity in a grain of sand. So he chose Mantis for his position at the centre of the circle of creation, although, or perhaps *because*, he was so small.

Consider for a moment the beginning of Mantis himself. For the Bushman, Mantis began in the ancient first soil of Africa as a tiny, invisible egg. That egg became a worm, creeping and crawling on earth before it was suddenly transformed into a creature of long legs and fabulous wings. Finally, in the act of procreation Mantis was devoured by his woman, that is, he laid down his life in the element through which alone he could create beyond his immediate self. The invisible beginning and the fateful end made the image complete in the mind of the Bushman. It is said in terms of living experience and behaviour that creation is not only birth but death as well, that through the death of what is, life on earth is born again to become more of what it is meant to be. If I had no other cause for believing that what the New Testament calls the Holy Spirit is the natural creative imagination of man, Mantis and what he evoked in the mind of the Bushman, and through the Bushman in mine, would be enough.

All this was implicit in Mantis's grown-up appearance. What sounds stark and horrific, perhaps, expressed as facts of knowledge out of the primeval African context, was conveyed with a certain rough sort of poetry in the impact the hieroglyphic shape of Mantis made on one's senses. For instance, seeing him as I saw him first in the grass of a high-veld summer, an immense empty blue sky above and a silent vacant plain, blue and gold, around, I had no doubt that he was charged with wonder. I was not surprised that Klara prayed to him. He sat there, absorbed in an attitude of complete reverence, his strange head always a little on one side to the wind as if waiting for it to bring to his listening ear the still small voice of the first spirit. With all that, there was something curiously human about his face. Its heart-shape, pointed chin, high cheekbones, and yellow skin – I realize now how like a Bushman's that face was. Besides, his eyes were extraordinarily big and bright, as if capable of extra-perception.

A wise and liberal theologian, who towards the end of his life was prosecuted for heresy by his church in South Africa, told me once as a boy that the word for sin used in the earliest Greek text of the New Testament was an archer's term meaning to miss the target. In this sense the Bushman was without sin. At heart he was a hunter not of big game but of greater meaning. It was the first spirit in Blake that made him cry:

> Bring me my Bow of burning gold!
> Bring me my Arrows of desire!
> Bring me my Spear!
> Oh clouds, unfold!

It was the first spirit in the Bushman that made him aim his imagination at Mantis like an arrow from his beloved bow, flying straight at dawn towards the game of the great plain around him. But in praising him, let us not forget, as he would not have forgotten, to praise also the insect.

13 Homesick for a Story

It is impossible to appreciate what Mantis meant to the first man without knowing something of the role which the story played in his spirit. The story was his dearest and most treasured possession. At the Sip Wells, for instance, I had found that the Bushman would share his most valuable belongings with us – his water, his food, and his knowledge of the desert. But the moment I asked him to tell me a story, he was instantly on his guard, pretending he had no idea what I was talking about. It was only after many days, when he had come to trust us more, that he confessed to having stories and told us some of them; but even so I always had a feeling that there was deep in his heart a story of stories which needed far more time and sharing of experience to communicate than I could afford just then.

The more I saw of him and the more I thought of the history of the encounter between Europeans and the first peoples of the world, the better I understood and respected his reticence. For the story was the greatest of his containers of first spirit; it was like the basket wherein his own lady of the starry sky stored the rare and dynamic intimations of his soul. Unlike that primitive man who lost his own lady because he lifted the lid of his basket and declared it empty, the Bushman knew his own was filled to the brim with things without which his life would have no meaning and his soul wither and die. He knew intuitively that without a story one had no clan or family; without a story of one's own, no individual life; without a story of stories, no life-giving continuity with the beginning, and therefore no future. Life for him was living a story: he kept the lid of this particular basket firmly shut, out of fear that some superior stranger, lifting the lid, would steal his treasure, either by persuading him into believing that the basket was empty or making a mockery of what he saw within it. He had good reason for fear.

We Europeans in Africa, America, Australasia, and the South

Pacific have been great stealers of the stories of first peoples. We have killed off whole races by taking their story of creation from them. Worse, the men whose speciality the first spirit of life is supposed to have been, such as the Protestant and Jesuit missionaries who preceded trader and soldier, rivalled one another in laughing at the most sacred stories of the first peoples and dismissing what they found in them as mere superstition and abominable idolatry. I myself confess to my shame that, though I have loved stories all my life and telling them is my trade, seeing the delicate concern with which the little Bushman stood guard over his story, I felt rebuked.

How much nearer to the truth seemed to me the old Bushman who described his emotions about the story to Bleek. I give his name and the little I know of him because I believe he should be remembered with gratitude for teaching us something we did not know before. Moreover, though he had suffered much, he passed on his one small lesson without bitterness. His name was Xhabbo: it is the Bushman for dream. When Bleek discovered Dream he was in convict's clothes, working a sentence of the hardest possible labour on the breakwater in Table Bay, because when hungry he had killed a springbuck of the veld on the property of a man who had stolen all his land. To Dream we owe much of what we know of Mantis, as well as these sentences which to this day must rend the heart that contemplates them: 'Master, thou knowest that I sit waiting for the moon to turn back for me, that I may return to my place; that I may listen again to all the people's stories . . . that I may, sitting, listen to the stories which yonder come, which are stories which come from a distance. . . . For I am here, I do not obtain stories. For I truly think that I must only await the moon; that I may tell my master that I feel this is the time when I should sit among my fellow men who walking meet their like. They are listening to the stories . . . I must first sit a little, cooling my arms, that the tiredness may go out of them . . . watching for a story I want to hear . . . while I sit waiting that it may float into my ear.' Though there might be mountains in between, he said, and though the road was long, yes! the story there would come floating to him. Listening, he would turn about in his spoor to feel in his ear the story that is the wind.

This is only a sample of one of the most haunting utterances from the past of my country, but it is enough to show where the real nostalgia of the spirit lies. More than homesick for 'his place', more than homesick for his fellow men 'who walking meet their like', he was homesick for his story. With such a fine regard for the property of the story, it is no wonder that everyone who knew him intimately in the past said that the Bushman was one of the greatest story-tellers of all time.

He had a story about everything. Even in my short acquaintance with the remnant of his race in the Kalahari, I learned that, close as his state of participation with nature was, the differences between one thing and another were all honoured in a story of their own. The fact, for instance, that the hare unlike any other animal had a split lip, was acknowledged in a special story. The hare, he

Hare

said, when a person of the early race was sent by the moon to tell the people on earth that 'as I in dying am renewed again, so shall you dying be renewed again', either did not believe it or got it wrong and told the first men on earth, 'The moon says that, unlike it who dying is renewed again, you dying will not be renewed again.' So angry was the moon with the hare for this fatal mistake that it beat him on the mouth and split his lip. Ever since then, the Bushman had only to look at the hare's lip to be reminded that death was not intended to be the end and that the spirit who would have it so was bearing false witness. Perhaps it was because of this split that hares were so confounded by the re-beginning of spring that they went mad. The hare contradicted the moon, the Bushman told Bleek, and therefore was condemned to have no shelter among the bushes of the veld, just as the spirit which rejects renewal through death has none. For ever after he lay in bare places where the vermin attacked and bit him.

Then there were the trees of his world. The differences between them were extremely important to him, as they were to most primitive people. He knew them all separately through this extraordinary capacity of his to participate in their nature, as if when observing a tree he in a sense became the tree, and through this process of becoming arrived at his conscious knowledge of it.

I myself had once observed a startling example of the negative aspects of this process in central Africa. I was deep in the bush with a large number of African bearers, walking faster and longer than I liked, because the rains were closing in on us fast and soon would make travelling well-nigh impossible. I made my camp much later than I normally did, in a sultry and ominous twilight by a group of extraordinary looking trees. They had trunks of an astringent sulphur colour and branches covered with a reluctant pointed leaf of an oily black-green colour. They made me uneasy. I was not surprised at my bearers being so affected by these trees that they made camp under protest. One bearer, who had once had a little schooling at a mission station, teased the others all evening long for feeling uneasy about 'mere trees' and upbraided them for being so superstitious and ignorant. In the middle of the night I was woken by a great clamour and found that the mocker of the evening before had been trying to commit suicide by hanging himself from the branch of one of the sulphur trees. His 'superstitious and ignorant' companions had rescued him just in time. When I asked him why he had tried to kill himself, he said: 'How could I help it when those trees all night long were telling me to hang myself from that one there?' He would not rest, nor did I feel he would be safe, until we had cut down the culpable tree. As we did so my head-bearer assured me that it would not have happened to the man if he had not mocked the trees.

The Bushman interpreted nature by means of story. For instance, on the northern fringes of his desert world he considered the baobab tree and how it grew. Livingstone did so too, dismissing it as 'a carrot planted upside down'. But the Bushman traced back its extraordinary appearance to an event in the beginning. When the first spirit was giving trees to the people of the early race he gave everyone something to plant and had only one tree left when the hyena, the force of evil, arrived. The hyena upbraided him, saying: 'Are you surprised I behave so badly when you treat me so differently from other creatures.' The first spirit promptly gave

Baobab tree

him the last plant, which was that of a baobab tree, and out of spite the hyena planted it upside down.

Again, on the great swamp along the northern frontier of the Kalahari, the Bushman saw the hippopotamus daily emerge from the steaming waters and, unlike other animals, scatter his dung with a vigorous movement of his tail to fall spread out on the earth. He had a story about that as well. He said the hippopotamus in the beginning begged to be allowed to live in water, which it loved more than earth, sky, sun, moon, or stars. It was told no, because with such a big mouth and such teeth it would soon devour all the fish. It promised it would eat nothing while in the water, and would emerge at night to graze on the grass and plants of the earth. Still it was refused permission, until finally it contracted to come out daily from its beloved water and scatter its dung, so that all creatures could test its good faith by examining the dung for fish-bones.

So close was the Bushman to nature that he not only marvelled over its manifestations and feared its power, but could also laugh with it, as a child with its mother. For instance, I had noticed for many years in the Kalahari that the ostrich almost invariably laid one egg outside its nest. I would find a nest with as many as thirty-three eggs in a close elliptical pattern in the warm sand, and then

The hippopotamus emerged daily

one shining egg well outside. I had debated the phenomenon with my friends, white and black, on many an expedition, and arrived at no satisfactory conclusion: but when I mentioned it to the Bushman in the Kalahari, they were helpless with laughter for quite a time before they gave me their answer. Did I not know the ostrich was a person of the early race, and such persons often did the most extraordinary things? The ostrich in particular was inclined to be absentminded, brooding over a precious thing which Mantis had once stolen from it, thus depriving it of the power of flight. He and his female deliberately put one egg outside the nest, to remind them when they were hatching that they were indeed sitting on eggs. Otherwise they might forget what they were doing, get up, and walk away.

In such ways the Bushman's stories stimulated his imagination, sharpened his sensibilities, and ceaselessly provoked his spirit to a greater awareness of meaning and time. The more I considered his stories, the more I discerned a clear and continuous pattern of greater creation in them. The pattern is transcendental and therefore beyond precise definition: it expresses itself through images which have to be described by words. Unfortunately, even for the most articulate minds of our day, the image is much more than the word, the colour, the sound, or the chiselled shape can make of it.

That is why the word or the dogma that claims sovereignty over the whole of the image, and does not often and humbly present itself before the image for renewal, in the end imprisons us. Yet I have no hesitation in saying that these stories and images, in their elements of wonder, of belonging and sharing, of laughter and tears, courage and fear, light and shadow, the end in the beginning and the beginning in the end, were an essentially religious pattern.

With Goethe I believe that the essence of religion is creation in man. As he said, 'Man is only creative when he is truly religious; without religion he merely becomes repetitive and imitative.' These stories, perhaps the oldest we have, coming as it were warm from the lips of the nursing spirit in the first nursery of the world, seemed to me to prove it. If religion is, as I believe it to be, the longing in the human being which encourages him to create beyond himself a new, greater expression of life and human personality, then the first man of Africa was remarkably religious. He had through his stories a design which, linking him firmly to the primordial origin and continuity of life, made him aware of the

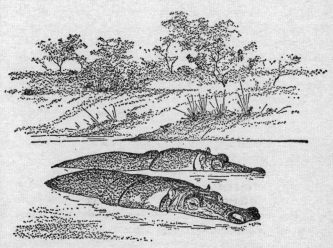

They begged to live in water

inadequacy of any static condition of being. Through this increasing awareness, particularly in the story of Mantis, he discovered in himself the power to achieve a greater and more authoritative, a finer and more accurate statement of life and personality on earth.

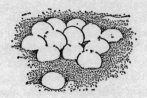

14 The Saga of Mantis

Mantis, the insect, as I have described him, is married to Kauru, the dassie or South African rock-rabbit. They appear to have had three children – a little daughter, a son killed in the Great War with the Baboons, and Young Mantis. Of the daughter I could discover nothing except that she had existed. Young Mantis, happily, is very much there in the story of stories. Besides the children of this curious union Mantis has an adopted daughter, the Porcupine, the child of another great character in the saga called the All-Devourer. Porcupine is married to someone called Kwammang-a who, more bewildering still, is not even insect or animal but something seen in the rainbow. Somewhere there is a hint that, despite his intangible substance, Kwammang-a was a son of Mantis's sister. Anyway, he and his bride the Porcupine are dear to Mantis and live with him, They have two children – young Kwammang-a, who is brave and quiet like his father, and the young Ichneumon, the mongoose, who is a great talker, calls Mantis grandfather and is always lecturing him on his foolishness.

Then there is the blue crane, that elegant bird which still curtsies to its own trembling reflection in the diamond water of the vleis of my home. She is Mantis's sister. Another sister, species not defined, is the mother of Mantis's special pet, a little springbuck. When I first contemplated this intimate circle of Mantis, consisting thus of an insect, a rock-rabbit, a porcupine, something out of a rainbow, a mongoose, an All-Devourer, a blue crane, and the issue of their various unions, I confess I was dismayed. I felt certain there must be meaning in these fantastic combinations, but on the surface they made no sense at all. For once I was almost glad that I had access only to a scrap of the saga of Mantis: the whole might have overwhelmed my limited capacity for understanding, since there are many hints that Mantis in the full story had a relationship with the early life of Africa as complex as it was vast.

I had one clue – the Mantis family were all people of the early

The blue crane

race. I took this to be the Bushman way of saying that they all represented aspects of the first spirit in men. Then my task became easier, for the insect and the animals round him were familiar to me. I could almost claim to have known them socially, as Mantis did, when I was a child, and to have participated in their being, as the Bushman participated. Once I had accepted the fact that their presence in Mantis's life was not accidental but had a definite point, I referred them back to my childhood experience on my mother's and my grandfather's farms, and was able then to link them with my grown-up thinking. Before long, I arrived at what I believe to be their contemporary idiom and human equivalents. The whole suddenly made immediate sense. This sense will emerge, I hope, as we come to each character in the unfolding of the tale.

To begin with Mantis. We meet him already established on earth and with a long history behind him. We know that he has for many years been the spirit of creation, the meaning, the dream made flesh. He is the image of the great togetherness of life and time, of the whole which our existence on earth experiences only in part. As time goes on he becomes, however, more and more the image of the differentiated part on earth striving towards a more meaningful reunion with the whole from which it came. One of the very first stories about him made a special point of his significance as a symbol of the spirit of wholeness in life. Once, the story says, Mantis appeared to the children of the early race as a dead hartebeest. This animal was particularly dear to Mantis – all Bushman stories emphasized the fact. In some stories Mantis appears actually sitting between the horns on the hartebeest's head, in others, more significantly still, between the toes of the hartebeest, as if demonstrating to the Bushman that the way the hartebeest walks through life is Mantis's way. 'Mantis,' the little Bushman said, 'did not love the hartebeest a little, he loved him dearly.'

One reason why the Bushman bestowed this highest of honours on the hartebeest was that his long neck and fine head rather resembles the mantis, just as the mantis's insect-like face resembled the Bushman's. This resemblance is clearly brought out in Bushman paintings on our rocks. Another reason, I am certain, was that the hartebeest was, in the high society of the animals of Africa, among the highest – his status equivalent to the Bushman's. He never moved in great herds like the wildebeest or springbuck or the black man, but in small selected family groups like the Bushman. He was one of the most cultured and civilized of animals, surpassed by only one other, the eland whom we meet later: it is as if, in exalting the hartebeest thus, the Bushman's imagination was quickening his own spirit to become the human equivalent of what the hartebeest was among the beasts of bush and veld.

The impression is confirmed by the knowledge that Mantis always carried a hartebeest's skin with him. At moments of danger and other great crises he would wrap himself in this skin; in other words, he would dress his spirit in his own natural attitude and find succour in his own vivid instinct and intuitions, of which the hartebeest was the glittering symbol. When the children of the early race discovered the hartebeest lying dead on the veld, though amazed that it had no wounds and was in perfect condition, they cut it up, rejoicing at the good feast ahead of them. But on the way home strange things began to happen. The girl carrying the animal's severed head suddenly finds its eyes open and winking at her. In alarm they all drop their parts of the carcass. Again they try to take up their loads, and again uncanny things happen; the dead head even whispers at them. They drop their loads, and before their frightened eyes the severed parts of the animal reassemble.

'The flesh of Mantis,' the Bushman said, 'sprang together, it quickly joined itself to the lower part of Mantis's back. The head of Mantis quickly joined upon the top of Mantis's neck. . . . The thigh of Mantis sprang forward like a frog; it joined itself to Mantis's back.' And so on, until the children can bear it no longer and run home. When, as a child, I heard the story beautifully read out from Bleek's rendering, I too felt like running for my mother. Today my imagination is still excited by the story, because it demonstrates Mantis as the spirit of wholeness in life, the element which joins the dead part to a living whole and is active in the apparent death of things. It shows too the Bushman conviction, so important to the understanding of his story, that matter and spirit are mysterious manifestations of one and the same whole.

The paradoxical character of Mantis as a differentiated part of the whole we know in the first place from the fact that he was the bringer of fire to the earth – 'old Tinderbox', as the Bushman called him. What the coming of fire meant, what it still is to primitive man, we do not fully understand. Some time ago, speaking at a university in Europe, I heard two senior students discussing fire. One asked: 'Tell me what fire means to you?' The answer came pat from the other. 'Why, energy of course.' The answer filled me with dismay, and I thought: 'That is our civilized way. There stand our arrested modern selves. Fire has become mere energy to us, a commonplace thing impressed in grates and boilers to raise steam for our "dark satanic mills" and set the impersonal wheels of our time turning. But to the first spirit, to the eternal primitive, it is a great many other things before it becomes that. It is the only light in the dark, it is safety against the danger that prowls by night, and it is life-giving warmth against the cold that would kill.' To us, it is the greatest image of the living awareness, the light of mind in man. This was Mantis's gift to man, for which he too had Prometheus-like to suffer.

Bleek has not recorded how Mantis brought fire to the earth, but the Bushman in the Kalahari had their version of what occurred: he stole it from the ostrich. Why the ostrich? I asked myself this sort of question at the appearance of every new character in the Bushman's story, because by this time I had the greatest respect for the precision of his imagination and believed that, if he chose an ostrich for a certain role, he did so because no other image could do the job so well. The answer, for me, is that the ostrich is the greatest of all birds and fire the greatest inspiration ever given to man. Over and over again I have found in primitive myth that birds represent the intuitive vision, the creative thought in men. Even Plato compared the highly organized classic mind to a cage of birds.

One of the most moving stories I know is the story of a hunter's quest for a bird. I heard it from a Hottentot servant on the Mountain of the Wolves, when I was a boy. There my brother and I on the long cold winter nights would invite this old man into the room we shared. Once upon a time, he told us, a hunter of the first people went to a place of reeds and flowers and birds singing by deep water. He knelt down to fill his calabash with drinking water, and as he did so was startled to see, in the still glass of the shining surface before him, the reflection of an enormous white bird that he had never seen before. Astonished he looked up, but the bird had already vanished over the black tops of a dense forest – 'the forest of the night'. From that moment his heart was filled with a restless longing to capture the bird.

Leaving his cattle, his wife, his children, and his people, he went deep into the forest looking for the bird, and out into the great world beyond. Yet everywhere he found nothing but rumour of the bird. At last, when he was a very old man and near his end, he was told he would find the bird on a great white mountain in the heart of Africa far north of his own home. He found the mountain and started climbing it. He climbed for days until, one night-fall, he found himself on the edge of the white cap of the mountain. And still there was no sign of the bird. He realized his end was near. Feeling he had failed he threw himself down like a little child, crying: 'Oh! My mother! Oh!' Then a voice answered him and said: 'Look! Oh! Look!' He looked up and saw, in the red sky of a dying African day, a white feather falling slowly down towards him. He held out his hand and grasped it. With the feather in his hand, he died content as the night fell.

'But what sort of a bird was it, old father?' we asked the shepherd. We often asked it; but always he would shake his head and say: 'I do not know its name; no one knows its name. It was a great white bird, and one feather of it in the hand of a man was enough; one feather of it on the head of a chief brought happiness to all his people.'

Afterwards I thought I found the answer in a similar tale told by the great and good Olive Schreiner. There the bird is called by the abstract name of truth. Since she spent her childhood in the village where I was born, I wondered whether she had the story from a similar source. At any rate, her story and the old Hottentot's seemed to confirm my interpretation of the role of the bird in the general imagination and in the story of Mantis.

According to the Bushman, what first drew Mantis's attention to the ostrich was that the place where it ate its food always smelt exceptionally good. One day Mantis crept close to the ostrich while it was eating and saw it for the first time roasting food on fire. When the ostrich had finished eating, it carefully picked up the fire and tucked it deep into the pit under his wing. Just as the sun issued from the armpit of a man in the early race, so fire came from under the same place of an ostrich. Mantis immediately realized the advantages of fire and wondered how he could get it from the ostrich. For days he went about, scheming in his mind. Already the vision of fire was teaching him to think. At last he hit on a plan – a plan designed grossly to betray the trust of the ostrich.

We must accept it that conscious intelligence in the first spirit produced a capacity to trick, deny, and lie to the primal urges of life: indeed, it evolved from acts of disobedience to them. That is why in mythology the bringer of fire is represented as a thief, and why Mantis in the first man's conception of consciousness is nothing if not a trickster and a liar. It was through his future self – through the son of his adopted children – that he would learn the importance of conscious obedience to truth as successor to the obedience he had once known to the first images of life.

Mantis now went up to the trusting ostrich and told it: 'I have found a tree with the most wonderful fruit on it; a kind just made for the taste of a person like you. Come with me and I will show it to you.' He persuaded the ostrich to follow him to a tree in the desert on which grew the lovely yellow wild plums that the gourmet elephants to this day walk a thousands miles in the rainy season to savour. The grateful ostrich began eating at once, but Mantis said: 'Pick your fruit with more care. Eat higher up; the tastiest ones are at the top.' The ostrich reached higher and higher, but still Mantis urged it on: 'You silly person, that's not high enough. Look at that yellow one shining up there. It is the grandfather of them all.' The excited ostrich stood on tip-toe, opening wide its wings to balance itself as it tried to get at the exalted fruit. At that instant Mantis snatched some of the fire from underneath its wing.

168

The elephant: titan of his world

Before that moment the ostrich flew; afterwards, the bird never flew again, lest in opening its wings for flight it should lose the little it had left of fire.

The greatest of first inspirations had come to earth for good. But Mantis himself had to suffer dearly for acquiring the fire. In the desert story he was destroyed in his own fire, as he was in the act of procreation as an insect, and his own wife refused to save him. Out of his ashes and bones two Mantises were made who bear a striking resemblance to Kwammang-a and Ichneumon in the main saga. One was soft-spoken, built shelters, and tended to withdraw into his own spirit when danger threatened; the other was bold, enterprising, and cheerfully went out to meet any peril in the external world. Here already we have basic images of the introvert and extrovert, the spirit that would contain and the spirit that would transform. If there were any doubt still that Mantis was the seed out of which grew consciousness and a greater awareness in the Bushman, it is confirmed by another statement to Bleek – that Mantis was the one who gave places and things their distinctive names; with Mantis came the word.

One of the first acts of Mantis and his children was to deal with disproportion in the great first urges of life. Now the great image of exaggeration and brute power in the Bushman's world was the elephant. In India and the East the elephant is a symbol of wisdom, of the triumph of cooperation between the natural and the calculated in man. In the Bushman's world it was not so. The elephant was to him what the one-eyed titans were to Odysseus – images of the exaggeration and excess from which his spirit had to free itself if ever it were to become symmetrical and whole. So he made war on the elephants.

In a story told to Bleek, Mantis killed an elephant because it swallowed a small first thing of life, his beloved pet, a little springbuck lamb. He was feeding it with honey which he was digging out of a hole, devoting the sweetness of his nature to nourishing the tender and the small, when an elephant came along and swallowed the lamb. When Mantis discovered this he went after the elephant, entered it by the navel, going as it were to the origin of the monstrous, killed it from within and emerged with the lamb, to carry it to his home – that is, to give the small a permanent place in his spirit. Way back there at his home, his sister looked at the grass on the veld and saw the wind blowing over it: the wind was coming out of the East. 'Oh! people, look!' she cried; 'why is the grass blowing this way? The wind is where the Master told me it would be when he turned back, when he was coming home . . .' The wind, the spirit, was coming out of the East where the day is renewed after the night, to bear witness to the fact that Mantis, in rescuing the significance of the small from the tyranny of the great, had renewed life on earth.

In the desert the Bushman had a wonderfully robust account of the war on exaggeration. There the two young Mantises find themselves saddled with an outsize elephant wife – a clear indication that the possessiveness of the first world of instinct was still too great in their life. They kill the elephant woman with the black and white quill of the porcupine. Black and white in the same shape are an image of the reconciliation of opposites in the first spirit of Africa: the significance of this weapon's coming from Porcupine, the daughter of the All-Devourer and Mantis's favourite woman, will emerge later. What matters here is that the other elephants soon heard of the deed and set out to kill the two young Mantises. The earth reverberated with the sound of their angry approach. One Mantis, the introvert, retired into the shelter he had built, as if to meet the danger through contemplation and prayer. The other sallied forth, met the elephants, jumped on their shoulders, and killed them in the most extraordinary way.

When the little Bushman in the Kalahari told me how, I could not at first believe my own ears. I looked at him and asked him to say it again. He glanced up at me, his eyes shining with the wonder of it, and solemnly repeated: 'Yes, indeed! He jumped on the shoulder of one elephant after the other, and farted in their faces. That was too much for them. One by one they fell over and died, until as far as the eye could see the earth was covered with dead elephant bodies.' He looked again at me, very serious, as if to say: 'Now, isn't that the most wonderful thing you have ever heard?' Then he became somewhat dismayed as laughter broke out from his listeners all around him: but soon the wonder that had shone in the story-teller's eyes possessed me too. I remembered that somewhere in a play of Aristophanes a naked man on all fours, his behind pointing to the sky, crawls on to the stage. 'What does he think he is doing?' one character asks. Another answers, pointing to the behind: 'It is learning to be an astronomer.'

I realized that in this act of Mantis I had a first image of the spiritual function of the sense of humour: it imaged that element of grace in us which corrects excess through laughter; the sound which accompanied the act, reproduced by the Bushman telling the story, was a sign that the body is digesting its food, extracting what is good and rejecting the rest, just as laughter is the sign that the metabolism of the spirit has extracted proportion from disproportion, rejected the waste in an excessive situation. This sense of humour became one of the Bushman's outstanding qualities.

Other delicate sketches of Mantis's concern for the significance of the small are seen in the Bushman's stories of the little striped mouse of the veld. Indeed, a battle of universal meaning is fought out between the mouse and the lizard, the mouse, and the black-beetle. In two of the stories recorded by Bleek, the striped mouse plays the same heroic role as 'Mighty Mouse' plays in the latest American cartoon; I am certain they both came out of the same secret hole in the wainscot of the spirit. I had asked myself – why a war between mice and lizards and beetles? The answer, after so many an exercise in the idiom of the first spirit, now came more easily. The lizard and the black-beetle of South Africa are two of the most earth-bound spirits it is possible to imagine. The black-beetle is a hustling busy-body, forever burrowing in the earth, blind to all but earthly considerations. Lizard and black-beetle have a daughter, who is held prisoner and compelled to do only their

171

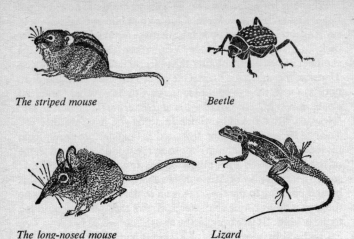

The striped mouse

Beetle

The long-nosed mouse

Lizard

earth-bound will. One day she sees the long-nosed mouse of the veld approaching. She exclaims: 'A man is coming!' Black-beetle and lizard at once scheme to kill him. They succeed, and then kill one long-nosed mouse after the other.

Had it been only a single long-nosed mouse, one might have thought the encounter accidental: but as it happens again and again in the story, it must be for a purpose. I believe it is because of the long nose of the mouse. The mouse in the primitive stories I know is an image of the ceaseless and invisible fecundity of the spirit. Indeed it is a symbol of the power of the small, despite the neglect or hostility of man's daylight mind, to stay alive and re-create in the secret recesses of his being – remember that wonderful Beatrix Potter story, *The Tailor of Gloucester*. The long-nosed mouse represents a particular aspect of this kind of creation. The nose is to the animal what intuition is to the spirit of men: it is the organ which enables the animal to detect what is far away and would otherwise be hidden. We say of a man who has good hunches in his profession that he has 'a good nose' for it.

Since the beginning of time there has been conflict between the spirit aware more of the future than the present and the spirit more aware of the present than the future. It is this war which rages between lizard, black-beetle, and the long-nosed mice. For long it

172

looks as if the lizard and the beetle, the children of this world far wiser in their generation than the children of light, will exterminate all the long-nosed mice on earth, and the soul, their daughter, remain forever bound to their will. Then Mantis has a dream. Over and over again we find that, when the final disaster is about to occur and life itself must fail, Mantis has a dream. Through the dream, he discovers what is wrong and what must be done. He sends the striped mouse into battle against lizard and beetle.

Now why the striped mouse? Because intuition by itself is not enough. Something is needed more in proportion than the long-nosed mouse – more differentiated and more complete. The striped mouse has a nose which, though keen, is not over-long: nor is he of one colour like the long-nosed mouse; his stripes show that he is not a one-sided character and is therefore a more highly differentiated spirit.

On the African veld this little creature, beautifully marked in dove-grey and black, is one of our daintiest and neatest. It moves amid bush and scrub, along tidy little runs and secret tunnels of its own; and though it has many powerful enemies, its senses are so acute, its ways so silent and mysterious, that it survives to procreate its species with astounding fertility.

The striped mouse goes into battle. He kills both lizard and beetle, exclaiming as he does so: 'I am, by myself, killing to save friends.' How moving this exclamation is at the end of a long and wonderfully detailed recital of the story! When the moment of deliverance comes and all the dead long-nosed mice are alive again, they wave the brushes made of hyena tails with which the Bushman of old kept flies from his face, and cry one by one to their striped deliverer: 'I am here, I am here!' Then all together this resurrected column of creation went home, the daughter – the soul free at last to follow its intuition of greater life – going with them. 'Walking beside her,' said the Bushman, 'was the striped mouse, for he felt that he was the husband of the girl.' And way back at their home, at the centre of the first spirit, Mantis, watching the wives of the long-nosed mice streaming out to meet husbands long thought dead, leans back, his restless spirit quiet for the moment, and somewhat overawed because he has accomplished all this through a dream. No wonder the Bushman told me 'There is a dream dreaming us.'

After the encounter with the ostrich and the theft of fire, Mantis had numerous adventures with other birds, other intuitive perceptions of reality. The pattern is always the same. Though he was never burned to death in fire again, he came to grief repeatedly by exploiting for a partial and selfish end some valuable piece of conscious knowledge he had gained from the birds. It was only through disaster that he learned how the conscious knowledge was given to him to serve also the source, the whole from which it came; he must observe the law of reciprocity between the conscious and the unconscious: the new food which the birds helped him to obtain for his spirit must be shared with them.

Kauru: the dassie

In learning this lesson the members of his immediate circle are called upon to play an important part. First of all there is his wife: Kauru the dassie, the rock-rabbit. She is what the language of dialectical materialism would call a social realist of the most uncompromising kind. I can vouch from my own experience that it would be difficult to find an African animal with feet more firmly on the ground. All day long she darts in and out of the shadows and clefts of our *kranse* and rocky hill-tops, a busy wife utterly dedicated to good housekeeping. She can have no particularly exalted role in Mantis spirit; all that is romantic and uplifted in himself seems to go to Mantis's adopted daughter, Porcupine; but Dassie plays a necessary part in his daily life. Physically, we know from the nature of her species, she must have been extremely fertile and have easily borne children. From the Bushman's story we know it was she who, when Mantis got into trouble with his neighbours, persuaded them to help him out of it. She represents the valid claim of worldly reality and community upon the attention of Mantis's spirit.

Mantis got into trouble so often, we are told, because of his tricks. This is not surprising, for to this day any new advance in individual awareness is resented by the conservative, backward-looking spirit of social man as a kind of trick or sleight of mind, if not a betrayal of what has gone before. Often in trouble with Mantis is Kwammang-a – that intangible character, the husband of Porcupine. Kwammang-a, we are told, is a rainbow element; and I myself believe that the rainbow is an image of the analytical, discriminating, reasoning aspect as it dawned in the first spirit of men. It was so to Goethe and it is so, I think, in the Bible, where it appears as the sign of God's covenant with man that the flood at the beginning will never be allowed to recur, which I interpret as meaning that the conscious spirit of man dedicated to God, to wholeness, will henceforth be strong enough not to be overcome by the blind, unconscious urges of life. The rainbow is chosen because it is the great white light, the whole divided into its basic colours, its hidden and constituent elements; it is thus the most exalted manifestation of natural analysis that we have.

Nor must we forget that Mantis was a kind of Noah and had to survive a flood at the beginning. He too needed some such arc in the sky as sign of the covenant of the first spirit that it would not recur again. With his conquest of fire and the achievement of consciousness, it seems to me right and inevitable that Mantis should have this rainbow element in Kwammang-a by his side. And the reason that Kwammang-a is so often in trouble with him is that he learns many of his tricks from this analytical element in himself, although he learns significantly enough neither their value nor their appropriate use. They both have to learn those from their future selves – Mantis from the grandson, the rainbow element from an aspect one degree nearer, his own son by Porcupine: this son, Ichneumon the mongoose, upbraids them both, his father by implication and his grandfather directly and constantly for foolishness.

How right that is too. We are all fools in the light of our future selves. Indeed we could not become our future selves unless we were prepared to let life make fools of us in the way it made a fool of Mantis. That is why the image of the fool, the clown, reaches so far down in all of us. Grown up, we tend to forget what we owe the fool in ourselves and neglect our own life-giving foolishness. We have to return to the memory of the child in us to appreciate the fool that brought us tumbling out of the dark wings of time into the light of the circus ring that is our brief round of life.

Whenever I read stories of Mantis coming home grieved and deeply injured by some new folly of his, to be upbraided by his future self, indeed by everyone except his beloved adopted daughter Porcupine, I think of the legend of a medieval fool in Europe. Day after day he performed his tricks in a great city so that the mob, too busy for foolishness of its own, too busy to live, could laugh over them. But at heart he was profoundly depressed because he had nothing nobler to offer life. One dark night he went for relief to pray in an immense cathedral. It was empty, and the thought came to him to perform his tricks before a statue of the Mother of Christ. He obeyed this impulse, going through his repertoire of deception and foolishness as diligently as if a great crowd were present. When he had finished, feeling more ridiculous than ever, he looked up at the statue; and suddenly it came to life; a tear rolled down her cheek and then she smiled upon him, as I believe Porcupine must have smiled on Mantis in his foolishness, otherwise he could not have loved her so.

Consider Porcupine, then: she is Mantis's own lady of the starry sky. When I first met her on the lips of a Bushman as an adopted daughter of an insect, I could not help smiling at such nonsense. I ceased smiling when I reflected on the nature of the porcupine because I soon realized how fitted she was in that world of first things to be the supreme expression of Mantis's intuitive soul. In Africa the porcupine is an animal that emerges only at night. Unlike the hyena she is a creative aspect of darkness: she does not go about to kill or injure any living thing, but merely to graze delicately under the stars on green grass and tender roots.

Just as the look in the hyena's eye tells one what its nature is, so does a glance into those of the porcupine. They are deep, dark, shining, and gentle, without a trace of aggression or confusion in them. They give her the power to see in the dark, as the soul gives men vision in its own dark night. She has a nose of great sensitivity and discrimination, the animal's equivalent of the intuitive and of true direction towards the future. Also she wears the colours of night and day – the uniform of the reconciler of opposites and the badge of wholeness: her quills are black and white, as a sign that even in the darkness she is bound also on a lawful occasion of light. I can only add that the Bushmen of the Kalahari had an unusually tender note in their voices when they spoke about Porcupine. They would describe almost with reverence how she was utterly at home in the dark and unfailingly found her way about. She would turn back to her home in a deep hole in the ground, they said, only when the Dawn's Heart strode, arrow to his bow, into the sky. As she crept into it for her rest, two bats would follow after and hang upside down from the roof, just where the passage turned to her room, to shield her gentle eyes from irritation by the desert day.

All I learnt about Porcupine convinced me that she is akin to the Ariadne whose thread brought man, after his encounter with the beast, safely out of the labyrinthine deep of himself – akin, too, to other aspects of spiritual beauty as presented to men in the shape of women, from Penelope and Héloïse to Laura and Beatrice. Indeed, in the last and greatest story of all, Mantis will turn to her as Francis Thompson turned to the same image in himself:

> Yea, in the night, my Soul, my daughter,
> Cry – clinging Heaven by the hems

Finally it must not be forgotten that Porcupine was the natural daughter of someone called the All-Devourer. Just as in the Greek beginning Aphrodite rose from the foam of the sea that swallows all, Porcupine came in all her star-stippled beauty of night out of the Bushman element that devoured all.

Of her two children by Kwammang-a, Mantis's discriminating rainbow element, the one who figures most in these stories is Ichneumon, the mongoose. He is the one who is always pointing out to Mantis where he has done wrong. Though Mantis is continually acquiring conscious knowledge from his rainbow element, Kwammang-a seems powerless to teach him how most creatively to use this knowledge. If life had been left only to Mantis and Kwammang-a, they would have had knowledge in plenty without any sense of how not to be destroyed by it. They would be in our own situation today, where humanity has more knowledge than ever before, and through this knowledge the nuclear power which threatens to destroy us all because we do not know how to use the power rightly. But in the concept of Mantis there is an element charged with this very task of saving knowledge from a fatal hubris and keeping it under control. This element is Ichneumon, the son of Porcupine and Kwammang-a, the product of the true Marriage of soul and mind.

Why should Ichneumon, the mongoose, be this image? Because in my part of Africa he is a creature both of the sun and the earth. He lives in deep holes in the ground but emerges to become a great killer of reptiles and snakes. I have seen him, no more than thirteen

Ichneumon: the mongoose

inches long from head to tail and perhaps only five inches high, take on a six-foot cobra. After a series of adroit and nimble feints wherein the snake repeatedly struck, to miss him by a bare millimetre, he would dash in, seizing the cobra at the back of the neck to bite instantly through its spine. A friend of mine had one as a pet, which saved our lives one day by leaping from the rug on which we were reading in his garden and killing a black ring-necked cobra that was about to crawl over us. In the wild he is a sociable, lovable animal, full of a sense of community and natural *gemütlichkeit*. He is intelligent, and if necessary as full of tricks as Mantis himself; but above all he loves the sun. His favourite position when not working for his living is to sit on his hind legs by his hole, bolt upright like a little man, enjoying the sun in company of his fellows. These qualities were enough to make him for the Bushman the expressive image of the element which joins the instinctive to the conscious, assimilates the snake and the sun, in the first spirit of men.

Finally, Ichneumon has a brother, young Kwammang-a, of whom we know little except that he was brave and quiet like his father. What we do know suggests that he represented an awareness in action, always a degree ahead of what Mantis could accomplish at any given moment. In the last story of all we shall see him playing a decisive role under direction of his mother, Porcupine, the first soul.

'*The people who sit on their heels*'

Thus equipped, Mantis set about his task of creating beyond his immediate self. It is most impressive how deeply this theme is woven into the stories of the Bushman: there is a constant emphasis upon life conceived not merely as *being* but also as an unending process of becoming. Here we find recognition of the fact that it is the element of becoming in the centre of his being that gives man's life its quality and meaning. The ancient paradox is asserted, in the lives of insect, reptile, animal, rainbow, sun, moon, and star, that he who lives his life merely to *be* loses it; he who loses his being in order to become lives forever. So Mantis, in order to become a greater expression of his own first self, finds he has to make war on the baboons or, as the Bushman called them, 'The people who sit on their heels'.

In those days everyone spoke everyone else's language – so much so that the Bushman who told Bleek the story of this war indicated that to tell it properly one should use the language of the baboons; however, he added respectfully, 'I must speak in my own language because I feel that the speech of baboons is not easy.' Now why the baboons? Because the baboon represents the critical mind in the world of animals; he is the intellectual, the high-brow, the representative of life as pure mind. Like most beings in whom the cultivation of the mind is the all-important consideration, the baboons are emotionally immature: any daughter of Porcupine at the age of three weeks would be ashamed of herself if she were not more mature emotionally than they.

This grave neglect of their emotional life makes them extremely touchy. Fond of playing tricks on others, they cannot endure having tricks played on themselves; loving criticism and all reductive processes, they can endure no criticism of themselves. They have a capacity for being insulted which I, who grew up with them, have never seen equalled in any other animal. As a result they have fewer friends in the natural world of Africa than any other creature except the snake. Moreover, like all beings who deny the urge towards wholeness in themselves, they are extremely neurotic.

'*Your foreheads resemble overhanging cliffs*'

There is a graphic account of their touchiness in one Bushman story where a man narrowly escaped with his life after saying to them: 'Ye! Speak to me! Ye are ugly! Your foreheads resemble over-hanging cliffs!'

All this is rather sad, because the baboons too have a valid contribution to make to the first spirit of things: their way of giving is through this very critical ability. It may be a pity that they are unable to use their great gift a little more on themselves, and that their idea of virtue seems to consist largely in pointing out what is wrong with lives they do not have to live themselves. Nonetheless, they have something to give. Mantis clearly realizes that he cannot enlarge his self without also submitting to the conscious critical faculties of life; in other words, without having the argument with the baboons of which war is the archaic manifestation. So he sends his son to go out and fetch sticks suitable for making arrows for his coming war. That the son should be an image of the father's future self seems to me obvious: but perhaps I should say that the Bushman so strongly felt the son to be an extension of his own personality that I have heard him scold a boy thus: 'How can you stand there in my body and not obey me?' The arrows for which the son has to find the wood are an image of Mantis's will to bring about a greater expression of himself. I think again of Blake's

> Bring me my Bow of burning gold
> Bring me my Arrows of desire!

This image of arrow and bow lay deep in the Bushman's mind. It was the first instrument of his own fashioning which enabled him to apply his will at great distances from himself. All that I know of him suggests quite clearly that it was not merely an instrument for obtaining food but also a creation of the spirit to him. He associated it as much with creation as with death. When I asked one of them how the idea of the bow came to the Bushman, he looked at me as if he could not believe anyone could be so ignorant, and would not bother to reply. When I persisted, he told me to look at the new moon in the sky and I would know the answer. I have shown later, in the story of Hare, how the moon was the great symbol of resurrection to the Bushman. The association of the bow with the new moon proves what a telling image of recreation it is in this story of Mantis. More, in the act of procreation the Bushman saw himself as a bow strung by the woman in his arms, the two of them together shooting a new life into the future. For this reason he still uses a cupid's bow in his courtship of a woman, as I have described in *The Lost World of the Kalahari*, finding it more eloquent than mere words for showing her how he longs to create new life through her.

Now as soon as the young Mantis has started to collect wood for his father's arrows, the baboons notice it. At once, as is the nature of the reductive spirit, they are suspicious. The oldest and most experienced baboon asks young Mantis what he is doing: it is significant that from then on the baboons refer to him as 'the child yonder'. The child, unfortunately, like every new vision of life when it first arises, is naïve and foolish to the point of self-destruction. Here one sees an early vision of the abiding pattern which has compelled holy men to behave in such a way that the word for a saint in many languages originally meant either 'lunatic', 'simpleton', 'silly', or 'idiot'. This association even extracted the word 'cretin' from the medieval French which described the village idiot as *un bon chrétien*, 'a good Christian'. Parsifal, who began the great adventure of the medieval world, was nothing if not simple. So too the young Mantis. It does not occur to him that baboons, so good at arguing with others, would resent an argument directed against themselves. He answers simply and truthfully: 'I am collecting sticks for arrows for my father to make war against the people who sit on their heels.'

The baboons quickly pass the news to one another, with rising emotion which, since they have neglected emotion in themselves, they do not know how to control. The highly emotional quality of their response is evident in the story as told to Bleek, for they talk

They play ball with the eye

about the presence of the child with that quickening of feeling we call poetry. Soon they cannot control themselves any longer. They fall upon young Mantis and kill him. They batter his head so that the eye falls out, and they can pick up the eye and play ball with it. If there is any better image of what the over-critical faculty, the

182

one-sided mind of pure reason, does to new creation, I have yet to meet it. The baboons go on playing ball with the eye, until baboon-like they each want to claim the ball, the vision, for themselves. The high emotion of all this is conveyed in a new series of poetic outbursts, baboon crying to baboon:

> And I want it,
> Whose ball is it?
> And I want it,
> Whose ball is it?
> And I want it.

When it seems as if what is left of the new vision will soon be destroyed in a quarrel among the critics themselves, Mantis, waiting at home for his child, has a dream. He dreamed, said the Bushman, 'that the baboons were those who had killed the child; that they had made a ball of the child's eye'. Through the dream, he sees what is wrong and what he must do to save the new vision. Indeed, because of the dream he can never be the same again. He acts with immense energy. With bow and quiver full of arrows he goes to the scene of the encounter so fast that the Bushman says he went 'rattling along, rattling along'. He has a tremendous battle with the baboons, is nearly killed himself, and only just gets away with the eye-ball of his son in the bag of hartebeest skin he always carries. I interpret this as follows: Mantis recognizes that the over-intellectualized, over-critical argument is killing both the new vision and himself: the only solution is to withdraw from the argument, protecting the new vision by the natural, instinctive attitude which the bag, the container of his beloved hartebeest skin, represents.

His way leads him to a place of water, grass, reeds, and green-growing things, an ever-recurring image of the source of first spirit. There he takes the eye tenderly from the bag and immerses it in the water, saying, 'Thou must grow out, that thou mayest become like that which thou hast been.' The source does not fail him. Day by day the eye changes, until Mantis, who visits the scene daily in great secrecy, hears it splashing in the water and in the end finds his child made whole again, lying in the sun by the water.

'Therefore,' the Bushman said, 'he gently came up to the child ... and he anointed the child with his own scent, and he said, "Why art thou afraid of me? I am thy father. I who am the Mantis,

I am here: thou art my son. I am the Mantis, I whose son thou art, thy father is myself.'' ' There, then, complete is the boy, complete the vision – the new way of life. There among the reeds of southern Africa is for the Bushman the way out from an arrested aspect of his spirit, as for the Israelites there was a way out of bondage in the child Moses hidden among the bulrushes of the Nile.

Bushman painting on bone

15 The Dawn's Heart

The Bushman lived in a state of extraordinary intimacy with nature. That, of course, was a characteristic of primitive life everywhere. Indeed the French observer I have quoted before singled it out as the main difference between the primitive and the civilized man, calling it a state of 'participation mystique'. Apt as the phrase is, it must not be allowed to conceal the difference also between primitive people generally and the first man of Africa in particular. This state of intimacy with nature seems to me to have been more positive and creative in the Bushman than among most other primitive people. In saying this I am aware how much this impression is exaggerated by the kind of picture of primitive life presented to us. I realize that it is the work in the main of people profoundly biased and already so far removed from the primitive in themselves that they could not really honour it in other men. I realize too that primitive society, by the time it came under European observation, was already either stagnant or disintegrating, and in Africa at least a society on the run for sheer life. What it was like in the beginning and in tranquillity we have slender means of telling. Such evidence as we have in myth, legend, and story suggests that it too knew a moment in the remote past when it was less distorted and imprisoned than when we made our first contact with it; but once contact had been made it never again got a chance of showing what it could have become.

Meetings of primitive and civilized cultures are events of extreme significance, with consequences of the deepest and subtlest import for both. Neither of them can be the same again afterwards. The European, arrogantly aware of his differences from the primitive, tends to believe that the consequences are only for the primitive and that he in his conscious superiority is immune from them. But actually there is no one-way traffic on these eventful occasions. The meeting with the primitive in the world without stimulates the primitive within the civilized. The civilized may reject it with the most stubborn determination, as he does in my native country, but the process goes on regardless. What happens is that, because of his rejection, the primitive enters his life secretly by some back door of his spirit. Instead of it becoming a positive factor, it becomes a negative, vengeful and destructive one, because he denies it the welcome of his heart and the service of his mind.

Yet, making full allowance for all these considerations, I believe the difference between the Bushman's intimacy with nature and that of other primitive Africans is real and important. The life of the Bushman was free from the tyranny of numbers. Nature, like civilization, has its heresies: it too has manifestations that would deviate from the main directions of life and seek to elevate a part of it at the expense of the whole. The first and oldest as well as most contemporary of such heresies, I believe, is the heresy of numbers. By the time we came into contact with primitive life in Africa, whatever it may have been before, it was firmly in the grip of numbers. Even to this day, what remains of primitive life in Africa is not free from that tyranny: one of the reasons the emancipated African so violently rejects tribalism and traditionalism among his own people is precisely that they still demand a disproportionate sacrifice of the one to the many.

The justifications for this development in primitive life are considerable and easy to understand. For example, it was only by combining in numbers that primitive society could hold out against its enemies in nature and man. Numbers gave it a power it could not have acquired in any other way, but a power which corrupted subtly. It made for bias, distortion, and all sorts of excesses and unrealities. Valuable and moving as it was, the reflection of the early reality in the imagination of the primitive world, because of this iron rule of numbers, was not so specific and precise as in the Bushman. He alone was never caught in this snare of numbers. Though the danger, as history shows, was greater to him than any of the others, he never appears to have lived the life of numbers.

Perhaps I should make it clear here that I have no desire to attribute any deliberate virtue to him in the matter. I do not want to imply that there was already in him a conscious intimation of the peril of numbers to the first spirit of life. But the fact remains to speak eloquently for itself: the Bushman's was a life of the few from beginning to end. It may have been so because he was a hunter who lived by the chase; my own excursions into life of that kind convince me that it can support man only in small numbers. Certainly the biggest Bushman community I found in the Kalahari numbered barely thirty in an area where game was plentiful, and I was told that was the standard everywhere in the desert. Though the numbers were bigger in the better-watered, more fertile valleys and plains of South Africa, I knew from history and the record passed down from lip to lip in my own family for three hundred years that the numbers were never great. Always the Bushman appears congenitally incapable of organizing himself in great numbers. Even the attempts of the few well-intentioned Europeans in my country to group him for his own safety in larger communities failed miserably. Nor did he learn from his enemies in this respect. It is true the European did not crush him with numbers. He did so because he had guns that out-shot the Bushman's bow and arrow and horses that out-ran him; but the tide of black humanity invading his country from the north extinguished him by sheer weight of numbers.

The Africans themselves were the first to admit that he had no equal in wit, skill, and courage. They feared nothing more than having to face him alone hand to hand: when near his shrinking areas, they moved about the veld in apprehensive numbers. Yet their example never seemed to tempt the Bushman to seek safety in numbers as well. To the end he was without concept of nation, although, as I hope to show, no one ever had a greater sense of kinship. One searches in vain through the rubble of the past that buried him and his magic for kings and queens or even chiefs. Such titles as 'Captain' and 'Chief', bestowed on him in our histories, were imposed by us in ignorance and from our habit of judging others by ourselves. He had no higher title to confer on his fellow men than 'grandfather' and 'grandmother', and he vanishes from the blue uplands of Southern Africa as he originally entered them – a hunter and not a peasant, an individual and not a collective unit, a man unique in his own experience of life.

In our era of vast numbers and unreal collective abstractions, the story of this first individual and his imagination is more important than ever, if only because it establishes that at the very beginning of things man was an individual, a hunter before a herdsman, the single Adam made in the image of the first spirit before the making of the many. Of all the stories we have of life experienced individually, this of the first man of Africa is the oldest and most sustained.

He lived then, this first individual, in a state of extraordinary intimacy with nature. There was nothing impersonal about his relationship with men and nature; he knew his fellow men personally, and he was personally and directly in contact with nature. There was about his life none of this cold, inhuman feeling that the existence of numbers inflicts upon the heart of the individual in our days. There was no sense of not belonging to the scene or being unrelated to the process of life around him – of that isolation which secretly eats away the courage and individuality of modern man. This sense of individual powerlessness or insecurity in the midst of millions, which paralyses the contemporary man, seems totally absent from his spirit. Armed only with his native wit and his bow and arrow, wherever he went he belonged, feeling kinship with everyone and everything he met on the way from birth to death. I myself would define his 'participation mystique' as a sense of being known; wherever he went he felt known, whatever he encountered, starlight, cloud, tree, or animal, knew him. I believe the Bushman's way to knowing was through what knew him.

When St Paul said, 'but then shall I know even as also I am known', he was drawing on that profound sense of first spirit from which the Bushman drew his own certainty of being known. We today, however, have no such feeling of being known. Man has never before possessed so much knowledge; but let him find himself suddenly on a hill-top alone with the wind or awake in the silence of the night, and he is terrified by a feeling of not being known, either by those dearest to him or by himself. This has the most tangible consequences, for it is only through our feeling of being known that we can value what we know and relate it accurately to life.

In the heart of the Bushman country where I was born, I have met examples of how the civilized person can be overwhelmed by this sense of not being known in the natural order of life. For instance, I was making a fire to brew coffee for myself on a great upland plain. The view was immense, the scene empty of houses and any other signs of men. Even the sky was empty of cloud: a great rain of blue light fell unimpeded on the earth, while a lean afternoon wind told the green-gold grass and sparkling bushes a traveller's tale of things to come. Then a cloud of dust appeared on the horizon and moved rapidly along the straight road towards me. Soon a car pulled up abruptly by my fire: a man I knew jumped out to ask me for help. He had his mother with him. She had come out specially from Europe to see him. Only ten days before I had met her in a big town by the sea. She was a lively, vigorous woman then, longing to see the interior of Africa. Now she had become a pathetic, pale person, frightened beyond reason or reassurance, begging her son to get her away from 'these terrible, empty, wide-open spaces'. I gave her a tot of brandy to speed her on her dash to the populous coast. Her son told me afterwards they travelled without stopping until they reached the sea, and that at one time he thought she would be suffocated by fear. I remember thinking even then: 'Emptiness without calls to emptiness within, and the emptiness within is the great plain in our spirit where our aboriginal feeling of being known has been extinguished as we extinguished the Bushman.'

How different the first man of Africa was. This sense of being known, of universal kinship was so great that he could speak of the stars as members of his family. For instance, he would address two of the most brilliant stars in the African sky as 'Grandmother Canopus' and 'Grandmother Sirius'. They were not remote, indifferent phenomena, but creative, active influences. My own eyes were opened that night in the central desert when I saw a young Bushman mother dedicating her newly-born child to a star. I had had an inkling then, which became clearer as the days went by, of how the human spirit and the stars conversed with one another. I possessed two words already which I was certain they had contributed to human vocabulary.

Both those starry grandmothers were associated with the abundance of 'Bushman rice', as we called the eggs of ants which were one of the great delicacies in his diet. On seeing Canopus, a Bushman told Bleek, he would say to a child, 'Give me yonder piece of wood so that I may put the end of it in the fire, that I may point it burning towards grandmother, for grandmother carries Bushman rice, grandmother shall make a little warmth for us; for she coldly comes out. The sun shall warm grandmother's eye for us.' He did this because the star appears at its brightest in the winter, and he believed that by offering it some of his fire it would offer and encourage the sun to offer them both the greater warmth which is necessary to produce his ant-egg rice. Sirius was an even greater wonder. When this greatest of grandmothers in the sky appeared, the Bushman would go about drawing the attention of his fellows to it. He invoked her in much the same way as Canopus; for hours he encouraged both stars with fire and song before he sat down content, feeling he had done his part – 'his work', as he said to Bleek – in putting them in the way of the sun's warmth.

Having slept out most of my childhood under the same stars that shone on the Bushman, I had my own guide to what such an association could mean. I knew Sirius well by sight and loved it best after the planets Venus and Jupiter, who alternately were our morning and evening stars and whose course through our cloudless skies I followed so closely that I could spot them in the blue at any hour of the day. From as far back as I can remember Venus entranced me and Jupiter exalted me; but Sirius, fat with light, reassured and warmed me between my blankets. Then one day, helping a coloured gardener dig out a nest of ants which were plaguing some delicate plants, I saw an ant-queen for the first time. She lay there on the black earth, a strange phosphorescent white, shapeless and bursting with new life. Observing her before the gardener could whisk her off, I was troubled by some memory I could not grasp. That night in my blankets on the grass looking up at Sirius almost straight overhead, so large and full of light that it was without shaft or shape, I knew what the unadmitted memory had been: the form and colour of the star in the night was that of the queen of the ants in the black earth. No wonder the Bushman could sing a prayer to her: 'For the star is not small, the star seems as if it had food. Give me of the heart of the star, that I may not hunger.'

Since the stars were also great hunters, the Bushman would ask them for some of their skill as well, praying to the appropriate star: 'Give me then also thy arm; thou shalt take my arm with which I do not kill. For I miss my aim. Thou shalt give me thy arm. For my arm, which is here, I miss my aim with it.' The heart of the hunter was the heart of a star, his quarry not merely the brilliant buck of the veld but also light in the darkness around him.

As he knew the stars, so did they know him. They knew him so well that they knew also the hour of his death, shooting through the heavens to carry the sombre news to others. 'At the time when our heart falls down,' said the Bushman, 'that is the time when the star also falls down, while the stars feel that our heart falls over as when something that has been standing upright falls over, on its side. Therefore the star falls down on account of it.' So great was this sense of kinship that he believed many of the stars were people of the early race. Indeed the sun, all animals, birds, insects, and even trees and plants were once people of the early race.

Some of the stars were made by persons of the early race. A girl, for instance, made the redder stars by throwing into the sky burning coals of a rich, red, scented, and nourishing root. She too made the great wonder of the night sky in Africa, the Milky Way. Like so many a Bushman act of creation, it came out of a moment of pain, isolation, and inner darkness. Alone in a hut, isolated because she was in transition between the child and the woman in her, hungry and bitter about her mother's apparent neglect, she put her hand in the wood ashes of her fire and threw them into the sky, commanding them: 'The wood ashes which are here, they must altogether become the Milky Way. They must lie white along the sky.' The story was told in full to Bleek with its own strange sort of moon beauty and this intimate reciprocity between the emotions of the suffering individual and the battle of star-light against darkness far out in the universe. Once the reciprocity is recognized the isolation is broken down: the suffering is placed in the procession of stars and life moves on.

From that day, said the Bushman, 'The Milky Way gently glows: while it feels that it is wood ashes. Therefore it gently glows. While it feels that the girl was the one who said that the Milky Way should give light for the people, that they might return home in the middle of the night. For the earth would not have been a little light, had not the Milky Way been there: it and the stars.'

So here at the very beginning, in a suffering feminine soul, the first spirit of Africa is joined in the battle for meaning. It has begun the painful task of making the universal specific, for in the imagery of the aboriginal language of the spirit that is what the girl does when she makes the Milky Way *her* creation. The immense labour of differentiation which is living awareness had begun; but differentiation, the image makes clear, is not mere separation as we tend to see it in our time; it is separation in order to establish firmer relationship. Most moving of all is the sense of exchange in the way the story is told. Not only does the girl 'feel' herself to be the lonely girl, but also the Milky Way 'feels' itself altogether to be the Milky Way. We shall come across this phenomenon over and over again in the Bushman imagination: there may be all sorts of inequalities in time, distance, and size in the various aspects of creation; but in the right to feel and fully to be what he is, there is for the Bushman no inequality. Here we have the aboriginal briar on which that great rose of the Christian spirit is grafted -- the axiom that all are equal in dignity before God.

Slight as are these fragments about the Bushman's love of the stars, they are greater than any I have encountered in the imagination of other primitive people in Africa. It has always been a keen disappointment and a mystery to me that the African imagination to which I owe so much took little account of our incomparable night sky. Few of the stars are named in our indigenous tongues, and on the whole the other primitive peoples of Africa have been content to acknowledge them only in their numbers. Not so with the little Bushman: in the beginning the stars, perhaps more than any other natural phenomenon, helped to correct the aim of his hunter's spirit, which he knew only too well to be fallible, and to send it flying like an arrow at a greater meaning.

It is, therefore, not surprising that his greatest star story is concerned with the morning star or, as he called it far more feelingly, the Dawn's Heart. The old Bushman father in the desert had

The Dawn's Heart

already described this star to me as the greatest of all hunters in the sky, saying that when it appeared the black night whisked about, the red dust spurting at its heels. In the imagination of the vanished Bushmen of my part of Africa the Morning Star was a hunter too, but it was also a person of the early race. As a person he had come down to earth, fallen in love, and taken as his natural bride the

The lynx: bride of a star

Lynx, also at that time a person. This marriage of a star to a lynx is perhaps the most inspiring example I know of the extraordinary precision of language which the first spirit of life forged in the fire of the imagination. If there is one animal among the multitudes shining like jewels in the grass, bush, and sombre forests of Africa more suitable than any other to be married to a star, it is the lynx.

In the Mountain of the Wolves, after which was named the great farm my grandfather gave my mother as a wedding present, there were several families of lynxes when I was a boy, and I had many an opportunity of observing them. I had even tried to make a pet of one, but I was forced to release it because it preferred dying to becoming reconciled to captivity. In its natural state, the lynx made an impression of flamelike grace, courage, vitality, and instinct which no other animal has ever equalled in my experience. When it appeared in the shadows far at the back of the cave where it lived in the Mountain of the Wolves, moving towards the daylight opening, it was like a lamp being drawn up from deep down in a dark well. Other cats may have been as vivid and as graceful, but they lacked the starry being of the lynx. The lioness, for instance, was far too big; the mere thought of her marriage to such a star offended the sense of proportion. The leopard was all that the lioness was and nearer the right size, but unfortunately she was spotted: the Dawn's Heart, pure in the stainless black sky of an early African morning, could not possibly have had a spotty bride. Only the lynx satisfied all the demands of shape, size, and unblemished fiery colour, so that when the marriage of the images was consummated, no wonder the Dawn's Heart loved the Lynx dearly and all other rejected females among the people of the early race were jealous.

Among these were the eaters of carrion, the accessories after the fact of sudden death, like the hyena, jackal, and the crow. The choice of the hyena as villain-in-chief is another example of this inborn regard for exact truth which characterized the first man of Africa. The hyena emerges out of its hole only in the hours of darkness. Although an animal of great strength and powerful jaws, it kills only the weak and prefers to live on the courage, initiative, and labour of others, scrounging what it can of the remains of the lion's or leopard's banquet. For the Bushman it was the most clearly accredited representative of the power of darkness and principality of evil.

Many a time, as I have listened to its wail alone in the night, miles from shelter and the sound of other men, I have thought of it as the cry of the damned and been troubled with emotions so far out of the range of my awareness that I cannot shape or name them. But

South African crow or raven

once I did have an encounter with a hyena that taught me much. The hyena had obviously overreached its capacities in the night and was caught by daylight on the way back to its hole. Its eyes designed for the dark could not see far or clearly, and as I happened to be stalking a Kudu I had made no noise that might have alarmed it. It passed within two yards of my position in the grass with that ashamed, fearful, loping movement and that constant over-the-shoulder glancing so characteristic of its kind. As it passed, it caught my scent. Fortunately the wind was blowing from it to me and the scent must have been exceedingly faint. Uncertain, it stopped to sniff the air between us. For a minute or more I was looking, for the first time, into a hyena's eyes. They were the saddest, most hopeless eyes I have ever seen in any living thing: I was quite unnerved by what they evoked in me. I no longer loathed the creature for all the terrible things I had seen it do to defenceless ewes and lambs and springbuck kids at home on the Mountain of the Wolves: I felt for it as one might for someone whose reason suddenly leaves them in the light of day and sends them down into the pit of loneliness and darkness we call madness.

It says much for the Bushman's imagination that even in assigning this unsavoury role to the hyena, the sense of kinship never abandoned him. He did not fall for the temptation to judge and to condemn, but observed the mysterious law of proportion as scrupulously as did Shakespeare when he honoured even Iago's

195

peculiar validity at the climax of his villainy. Indeed, I know another Bushman story of the numerous encounters between hyena and lion, in which the lion has by far the worst of the exchanges because he refuses to honour the hyena's validity and lacks the humility which made a Christian spirit once exclaim: 'There but for the Grace of God go I!'

Kudu bull

Once when the Dawn's Heart was away hunting, the she-hyena bewitched the Lynx through the Bushman rice – the ant-egg food which we have seen already associated with other great stars and which she too evidently loved. The hyena did this by taking perspiration from her armpits and mixing it with the delicate food. This is the Bushman way of saying that the spirit of the hyena entered the food, the spiritual nourishment of the Lynx. I say this because food was never mere food to the Bushman. What a person ate, so in a sense he became. A Bushman father, for instance, would never give his son the meat of a jackal to eat because the jackal was

196

a coward and this would make the child cowardly too. He gave the child the heart of a leopard, as he gave its mind the heart of a star, because a leopard was one of the bravest of the brave and would make the child brave.

So it was throughout the primitive world: as one ate so one became. I know Zulus who to this day will not eat fish lest the diet should turn their warriors' hearts to water. But this taking of perspiration from the armpit to put in the lynx's food had a more than

The jackal

ordinary significance. The armpit was a source of special being to the Bushman; it was the place where the quintessence of living things issued. The sun, the source of light and warmth, the great image of the power and glory of reason, was once the armpit of a man of the early race. Thus man, baptizing his son into his own kind of manhood, took perspiration from his armpit and smeared it on his son's head. The she-hyena, in doctoring the lynx's food thus, is turning it into a concentrate of hyena spirit, a highly charged potential of darkness and evil.'

Immediately it takes effect. The ornaments fall from the lynx – first her earrings, then her bracelets and anklets. Then her skin cloak unloosens itself and slips down, her skin petticoat does likewise, and finally the thongs that tie her sandals to her feet break. Naked and screaming she runs away to sit among the reeds – that is, near water, which here is an image of the chaos life had to overcome at the beginning. This is the Bushman way of describing the approach of madness, the invasion of dark unconscious forces into the light and consciousness of man. The things the Lynx loses are all symbols of conscious manifestations of the spirit: the ornaments, of the art and grace in which it expresses itself; the cloak and petticoat, of the living thought wherein it daily clothes itself; the sandals, of its chosen way of life on earth. When the spirit loses all these, dissolution in the primeval water is imminent.

I was all the more certain of this interpretation of the story now, remembering the demented Bushman woman at Gemsbok Pan, walking naked and moaning like a hurt puppy in the burning sun, and Dabé saying to me, 'The time of the Hyena is upon her.' The imagery of this story of the Dawn's Heart and his bride gripped me like some Greek drama of the battle of a single soul against a dark fate that would overwhelm its conscious defences and so deprive it of clarity. So deeply does the Lynx fall under the Hyena's spell that her sister, the image of the natural love that is her last defence against isolating evil, has the utmost difficulty even in getting her to suckle her own child.

For a while the two sisters fight desperately against the growing power of the Hyena's spell, while the power of the child to entice the mother to come from the reeds and suckle it gets less and less. It is the Bushman way of acknowledging that in the eternal battle of the soul against darkness the great feminine forces of love, indispensable as they are, in themselves are not enough; feminine love, however great, needs male armour. So the drama draws to its climax. At last the Hyena, certain her time has come, moves confidently into the hut of the Dawn's Heart, pretending she is the Lynx. The evil now is ambitious; the aim is not merely to destroy the star's light of love but to turn its own clear shape to formlessness and darkness as well. At this moment all the forces in the battle are truly joined, the male element rallying to the female. In the final twilight, with love at bay, the sister of the Lynx tells the Dawn's Heart of the Hyena's grand design. He goes into action at once, drives at the Hyena with his spear: that is the Bushman way of saying that he hurls his precise, discriminating male spirit at the confusion, darkness, and fear implicit in the Hyena. He misses her, for it is in the nature of evil to be indestructible; but he does send her running away, so fast that she burns her feet in the fire outside the hut. Thus light and consciousness have left their mark on darkness and unawareness, making them more easily recognizable and somewhat less formidable for the future.

I like to think, as the Bushman did, that this is why the Hyena is still compelled to slink home through the first light of Africa with that strange limping sort of gait, as if its feet were still blistered from the burns of the fire, thus bearing witness forever to the power of love and courage to free the soul from the fear of life on earth. Certainly, for the first man of Africa ever afterwards, the Dawn's Heart was a sign as meaningful as the rainbow in the sky to Noah's descendants. It was for him, I believe, a token that the loveliest, brightest and boldest body in his sky is for ever alert against the subtle designs of darkness; that deep in man's inmost soul there is a shining element for ever protecting it against the chaos and old night that preceded the coming of the dream which, according to my desert hunter, was still dreaming the Bushman.

The hyena

Other mythologies, like that of the Aztecs, far more comprehensive and highly organized than the scrap left behind by the Bushman, have made much of the morning star, assigning it a significant role of mediation between the two great opposites in life, the night and the day in the spirit of men. They built up around this star a special imagery, which suggests that in its strategic position between night and day it was proof of some power which enables man to transcend these opposites in himself and so to reconcile them that they become greater than the mere sum of themselves. In doing this, they did what the Bushman did: they used the world without, I believe, as a great mirror wherein to see reflected what was hidden within their own natures.

At any rate, so the Bushman told Bleek, since that day of near disaster to his bride, the Dawn's Heart comes home in the morning vigilant, his eyes open and great with light, flashing so that the eaters of carrion turn about and run for their holes. Just in case the hyena has been up to her tricks again, the Dawn's Heart comes home fast, arrow at the ready, driving his spear into the earth with each long stride. Is there any great difference between the Bushman who could think of the stars thus, and Blake who in writing of that other cat, the tiger burning bright in the forest of the night, spoke of the moment

> When the stars threw down their spears,
> And watered heaven with their tears.

So the traffic of meaning between the Bushman and the stars has gone on from the beginning right into the lives of his descendants in the desert of today, like that traffic of angels which Jacob saw in a dream during his own desert flight, ascending and descending a ladder pitched between him and the sky. Nor was the traffic visual only. I have already mentioned the sounds wherein the stars speak to the Kalahari Bushman today; nearly a hundred years ago a Bushman told Bleek about their voices; and he said too – a thing I had not heard in the Kalahari – that the sun had a great voice of its own. It made a ringing sound in the sky. When I read that, I thought instantly of the great chord with which Goethe begins the music of *Faust*:

> Die Sonne – tönt nach alter Weise.

16 Sun, Wind, and Rain

This ringing sound of the sun had a particular significance for the Bushman. It was the supreme evidence of his belonging. As long as he could hear it, he was at one with life. When it vanished, it was a sign that he was deeply estranged and injured in his spirit. All this found utterance in a poem recited to Bleek. The poem was composed by the father of the Bushman who recited it. It was composed on the death of a friend, and the death itself is described in curiously Goethe-like terms. Goethe spoke about the *Gefühlsfäden*, feeling-strings, of human beings; the Bushman spoke of their 'thinking strings', and death for him was the moment when a man's 'thinking strings were broken'. Composing his poem then on the death of his friend, a great magician killed while going about his business in the shape of a lion, he begins by lamenting that since 'the string was broken' the sound which used to ring in the sky for him no longer rings. Here is the part of the poem which follows the lament:

> People were those who
> Broke for me the string.
>   Therefore
> The place became like this to me,
>
>   On account of it,
> Because the string was that which broke for me.
>   Therefore,
> The Place does not feel to me,
> As the place used to feel to me,
> On account of it.
>   For,
> The place feels as if it stood open before me,
> Because the string has broken for me,
>   Therefore,
> The place does not feel pleasant to me,
>   On account of it.

The Bushman's sense of intimacy with nature was as great by day as by night. He greeted Sirius as Grandmother; no less, he spoke of 'our sister, the tortoise' and even of 'our brother, the vulture'. Where the creatures and things of the first world are not actually blood relations, they are acknowledged as having been people of the early race. Lightning and thunder are still two brothers quarrelling and fighting each other, with a white lightning that merely hurts and a black lightning that is invisible and

'Our brother, the vulture'

kills. Even at the height of the storm – and only those who have experienced a thunderstorm in the sulking hour on the great upland plains and among the iron-stone boulders of his native country can know what that means – he found courage in this overwhelming sense of kinship.

From childhood he was commanded, when the lightning flashed near, not to blink but to open his eyes wide and look straight back at it, since he who acknowledged its share of their common reality would be acknowledged in return. He told Bleek: 'Even when the rain's thunderbolts have come near us, if we look towards the place where it has lightened, we look making the thunderbolts turn back from us: for our eye also shines like the rain's thunderbolts. Therefore it passes over us on account of it, while it feels that it respects our eye which shines upon it.' Lightning is the awareness, the revelation imperative, thunder the word of nature summoning the earth to awake and renew itself through the rain about to fall.

The wind was another phenomenon through which he felt himself to be part of the processes of life. Bleek was told several stories by Cape Bushmen of the images the wind evoked as it came blowing through the wood in the beginning. It too was, naturally, a person of the early race, but not an independent person. We meet it as a child, as a young first thing of life like the Bushman himself. When the child is standing upright, then the air is still and life is calm; but when he lies down, things begin to move, and when he starts kicking like a child on his back, things begin to fly about and life alone knows what would have happened, if he had not had a mother to pick him up and set him on his feet again and a father to build a hut wherein he could be put. Even as a person of the early race, therefore, he was a young thing with all life in front of him, an instrument of the natural love and authority represented by the mother and the father. Later on he became a bird which lived in a cave in a mountain, from which he issued when hungry to look for food and as the Bushman put it, 'to eat, about, about, about, and about'. Then, of course it blew. Whether it was a bird or a child, the relationship of the Bushman to the wind was so intimate that he felt it to be inside as well as outside him.

When he died, his own wind joined in the greater wind without to make clouds. This business of making clouds had a vital significance for him. Alive, he was convinced, he made clouds naturally out of what he was. On a hot day he would sit in the shade and, watching the cloud growing like a giant cauliflower in the blue, feel that his liver had gone from him to join in its making. Of all the many images I have of his indomitable little figure moving through the immensities of Africa, this is one of the most poignant. I myself know of no circumstances which make one feel more insignificant than finding oneself alone on a hot summer's day in the silence of the immense veld with the great clouds swimming above one in the blue like whales over a shrimp.

Yet even in that extremity of contrast, his spirit did not drag. He had none of that feeling of disconnexion which cuts like a knife through the heart of a civilized man and which made a friend of mine exclaim once: 'The trouble about life is that it is not a whole time occupation.' I am certain that these clouds were for the Bushman a reflection of the invisible processes of his soul fashioning the first active instrument of the spirit; that in fact there under a bush in his nakedness and isolation he was in the same natural state of grace as compelled Wordsworth to recognize that his own soul came neither in nakedness nor in forgetfulness but trailing clouds of glory from its home. Through the clouds and the wind the Bushman had similar intimations of immortality, and a certainty of being for ever known and remembered. For even in death and beyond, this wind within him, this movement of the spirit towards greater life went on participating in the daily business of living.

Yet before the wind made more clouds, it performed a last service for the man who had just released it. It made dust to erase his footprints, lest there should be any confusion about his going. His clear spirit demanded clarity in death as it exacted precision in life. So the wind rose, he explained to Bleek, 'because it intends to blow, taking away our footprints, with which we had walked about while we still had nothing the matter with us. And our footprints which the wind intends to blow away would otherwise still be plainly visible. For the thing would seem as if we still lived. Therefore, the wind intends to blow, taking away our footprints.' Once that was done, the wind within joined to the wind without was free to make clouds; even the hair of his head, in this manner, became clouds when he died, so much so that looking at the shapes of the imminent storm going up like an explosion in the blue, he felt they were 'a person's clouds'. 'We who know,' he said with unusual emphasis, 'we are those who think thus, while we feel that we, seeing, recognize the clouds, how the clouds in this manner form themselves.'

So the wind within was the same breath of life that breathed upon the invisible essences of water, light, and heat, gathering them and making them stand up living and vibrating with lightning and thunder in the blue, to join in a new act of creation on the world below. The wind was the ancient first urge of life from long before his own personal being, travelling on and on when the dust had been laid over his last spoor, for new acts of creation beyond. As Klara, my nurse put it, in a favourite riddle she had from her Bushman mother: 'Who is he who goes here, there, and everywhere, waking up the living and making the dead alive? Why, you silly child, he is the wind!'

One of the Bushman's tenderest stories is concerned with the wind's mission in matters of life, death, and resurrection. He had killed an ostrich, and he and his wife put some of the ostrich's bloodstained feathers on some bushes to dry, before settling down to eat the meat. While they were eating, a little whirlwind approached them and blew upon the ostrich feathers. Selecting one little feather with blood upon it, the whirlwind carried it up to the sky. 'This little feather,' a Bushman told Bleek, 'falls down out of the sky, it having whirled round falls down. It goes into water, it becomes wet in water, it is conscious it lies in water, it becomes ostrich flesh, it gets feathers, it puts on wings, it gets legs while it lies in the water. It walks out of the water, it basks in the sun upon the edge of the water because it is still a young ostrich. Its feathers are young feathers because its feathers are little feathers. They are black, for a little male ostrich he is. When his little feathers are dry he may walk, unstiffening his legs.'

I long to carry this sketch of re-creation to its end in the maturity of the little bird, because it trembles with the Bushman's quick love and delicate concern for the small young first things of life. Here, at any rate, we have images of the fundamental elements of re-creation. Life, confronted with death, is compelled to renew itself out of the insignificant and small: a little feather, a drop of dry blood, a departure from earth in a turning movement upward through light and air, and a return to earth through the water of the beginning. The vehicle which begins and completes this eventful round of departure and return is the wind. Perhaps the most compelling of all the images of the wind is this one of it spinning around the still centre of itself and aspiring in a tower to the sky, as it moves across the earth. Certainly it was a familiar feature of the Bushman's scene in the hot dry months before the rain, and no first storm of summer ever broke without at least one whirlwind striding in front of it over the scorched land like a giant carrying a torch of fire in his hand.

We who stole the stage from him watch these spiral winds with a strange, uninvited feeling of awe. Some of his and our own primitive associates even think of them as evil spirits, dust devils. Others see in them a manifestation of supernatural power about to take a hand in human affairs. The Zulu seer and prophet, who complained to me that men today no longer speak of the great first spirit of his people but only of things useful to them, saw the wind in this same primitive context of Africa much as the Bushman saw it. He told me that, ever since he could remember, the voice of the great first spirit of the Zulus had spoken to him. It had spoken to him in the sound of the wind in the grass when he first went out to herd the cattle with his brothers; in the song of birds at dawn and at evening, and the water rushing over the rocks in the bed of a stream. He heard it in the rain and listened to it in the thunder; but he did nothing about it until it spoke to him out of the centre of a whirlwind spinning over a deep, still pool of water in the heart of a silent noon-day Bush. It had commanded him then to do something which appeared to his thinking mind useless and stupid; but he let his spirit be raised by it, as the little ostrich feather was raised in the Bushman story, and he gave himself over entirely to obey the voice as the feather obeyed the movement of the wind. There and then his old life was dead behind him. He began a new life as a seer and a prophet, seeking to quicken the dead spirit of his land.

Between the primitive seer and the Bushman, between them both and the poet of today and tomorrow, the wind seems to bear forever the same imperative image: the wind rises and the spirit moves. If this were not so, how could Valéry have written:

Le vent se lève. Il faut tenter de vivre.

And how, otherwise, hearing those words, could we be so moved?

During my own journey in the desert I had heard the Bushman singing a song wherein the wind played its ancient role. It was all the more meaningful to me because it was a song about both the wind and the rain. This partner of the wind, this other great intimate in the Bushman's circle, was once a person of the early race. It visited the earth in the shape of a majestic bull to woo the young first woman. One of the Bushman's loveliest stories is concerned with a visit by the rain to court a beautiful young woman. The bull, restless with a longing to create and impatient with the lack of an element to receive and give shape to his longing, comes down to earth, moving through the mist of morning which is the mint of his own ardent breath. From afar he scents the fragrance of the woman, and unerringly the scent leads him to her. The woman at once recognizes the longing and the fever in him: she throws one of the most fragrant of wild Bushman herbs on his head; she shows in other words, that her feminine spirit recognizes that it is royally summoned. Quickly but delicately she lays her own child, her own personal love, aside. Europa-like she mounts the bull out of love of greater creation and guides him to a tree in a ravine where she dismounts and soothes the bull to sleep. When he wakes up he rises, believing the woman is still with him, and returns to his own element in the water at the centre of a spring; he becomes, that is, the male contained in the female, a fountain of creation of clear water bubbling out of the earth.

The story is told in loving detail, but I have given only as much of it as is necessary for understanding the song of the wind and the rain as the Bushman understood it. I heard it in the desert before the rains first broke the terrible drought at the Sip Wells, where I, ignorant as yet of the song and forgetful of the story of the bull, thought of the earth as a woman talking to the rain like a lover in her arms. The first time I heard it, a woman sang:

> Under the sun
> The earth is dry.
> By the fire,
> Alone I cry.
> All day long
> The earth cries
> For the rain to come.
> All night my heart cries
> For my hunter to come
> And take me away.

Then a man replied:

> Oh! listen to the wind,
> You woman there;
> The time is coming,
> The rain is near.
> Listen to your heart,
> Your hunter is here.

This linking of the dryness of the earth with the state of loneliness in the woman's heart; of the coming of the rain to the earth with the coming of the hunter for the woman, seemed to me now anticipated and explained in these Bushman myths of the wind and the rain. I cannot describe the reassurance I felt when I saw an unbroken chain from the earliest images to the utterances of our own desperate day. If it were ever broken, if this string too were cut, life itself, I have no doubt, would cease. But I do not believe that can happen. Whatever the disasters ahead, they would be designed, enigmatic as it may sound, not to destroy but to serve life. Whatever happens to a man himself, the wind in him – as the Bushman would have put it – will go on blowing to make clouds for new rain to fall.

Through the despised spirit of this vanished Africa I was brought to a new understanding both of basic truths and of the civilized processes of life. Here, for instance, I saw the reason why poetry, music, and the arts are matters of survival – of life and death to all of us, and why Blake's Bushman sensibility could perceive that, when the arts decayed, nations decayed. For the arts are both guardians and makers of this chain; they are charged with maintaining the aboriginal movements in the latest edition of man; they make young and immediate what is first and oldest in the spirit of man. When I thought of the past of Africa, in particular the history of man in Africa and the horror through which his humanity had come – a horror so great that the contemporary children of Africa will not own their share in it and are today busy, from Senegal to the Cape of Good Hope, inventing histories that never happened in order to sweeten it – I was reduced to a gratitude and humility I cannot adequately express before the little Bushman, who maintained unbroken his link in the chain.

It is no wonder that, so profoundly engaged in the vital continuity of creation, he seems to have acquired extra-sensory perceptions. I have already told the story of how, the day we killed the great eland, I heard for the first time that the Bushman had a system of telegraphy in his spirit. The Bushman told Bleek very much the same thing: 'The Bushmen's letters are in their bodies. The letters speak, they move, they make the Bushmen's bodies move. The Bushmen order the others to be silent: a man is altogether silent when he feels his body is tapping inside.' Bleek then describes some of the things this tapping told the Bushmen. For instance, it told them which way they were not to go, which arrow they had better not use; it warned them of the approach of strangers when they were still far away. Through this tapping, the Bushman claimed to be able to feel the presence of springbuck on the far side of a hill, so keenly that he was aware of the wind blowing through the dark hair on their flanks, and would say to his sons, 'Climb the hill standing yonder that you may look around at all the places. For I feel the springbuck sensation.' When an ostrich came near him, even when still invisible, and started scratching the back of its neck with its foot, he would feel the tapping in his own neck at the same place where the ostrich was scratching. When one of his own people was approaching, who he knew had an old wound, from afar he would feel a tapping in his own body in the place where the wanderer had his scar. If a woman who had gone away was returning home, the man sitting by her shelter would feel the tapping on his shoulders where the thong on which the woman's child is slung presses on her own. He even claimed that he received news in this way of the progress of a louse through the feathers of an ostrich.

The ostrich scratches his neck

Whether these claims were exaggerated or not, who at this distance can say for certain? I know only I had seen something approaching verification of the claim when the great eland was killed and the day we had that unexpected encounter with the desperate little band of Bushmen on the way out from the Kalahari. On this last occasion, when I asked Dabé how he knew strangers were approaching, since there was no visible or audible sign of them, he had significantly tapped on his chest and said, 'I feel them coming, here.' But whether the claim was literally true or not, this image of the event to come, tapping within the body of man, stands as evidence of that perception of the nature and shape of things not seen, which is one of the finest functions of the imagination.

It is moreover the first image which gave man his ideas of signalling news over great distances – the beating of messages on drums in the primeval forests of Africa, the ordered striking of bamboo gongs in the jungle silence of Java, or the electric tapping which is the morse transmitting an sos from the wireless keyboard of the sinking ship today. 'Only those who are stupid and do not understand these teachings,' the Bushman said, 'disobey the tapping in themselves.' How full our world, particularly my native world in Africa, does seem of fools who will not heed the urgent future tapping at their hearts? If only the clamour of words could die down in the world for a day and the modern man could be altogether silent, as the Bushman was commanded to be when he felt the tapping coming on in himself, he might hear perhaps his rejected aboriginal self, his love of life and element of renewal, tapping on his own back door.

This gift of the first man to perceive and to serve the life-giving image came out in his music, dancing, and painting too. Re-examining all these things, I remembered now the night I saw him dancing the fire dance at the Sip Wells with the first great storm of summer coming up – how he went round and round his magic circle hour after hour, like a whirlwind turning on its own centre and bearing a feather of life towards some water of renewal. I felt at the end of it, more than I have ever felt in any church, temple, or

Rock painting of a dance   *Zebra painting glowing on the black rock*

cathedral, that I had shared in a living experience of what theologians call God. I felt the same thing in the presence of his paintings burning in the shadows of some gorge or purple overhang of rock. I felt it when I watched him engrave abstract designs on ostrich egg-shells – triangles, squares, parallelograms, and circles worthy of the propositions in my own school textbook on geometry.

He even knew the importance of crossing himself. I was told that in healing his sick he often made a cross of the wood of some tree that was magic to him and laid it on the chest of his patients. I know of one rock on which he made his own sign of a cross, and I possess a copy of the painting which shows how his heart beat in his finger-tips as he laid the red colour of the cross on the yellow stone. It is, I imagine, one of the oldest crosses in the world. Thus his imagination in every way was composed of fundamental and

210

abiding imagery. His intuitive geometric shapes are the same on which is built the science that would throw a bridge across from island to continent.

Even today we have barely apprehended the meaning of these symbols which welled forth from his spirit. They recur over and

Abstract imagery painted on ostrich egg

over again in our own imagination, inviting us to deeper exploration of living behaviour. The image of the cross, in particular, remains a symbol of infinite mystery and power, as it was in the beginning of things in Africa, urging the first men to live not only horizontally but vertically as well. I would say, therefore, that another important difference between him and us was this: he was obedient to life and faithfully served his own first image of it, whereas we not only usurp and exploit the image but have fallen into the gravest delusion of the men whom the gods would destroy – the delusion that we have invented the image ourselves.

17 The Beautiful Eland

We left Mantis victorious over the baboons. He was now ready for
fresh acts of creation. The greatest of these was the act accomplished through the eland. It may seem strange that even at that
stage the first spirit was limited to accomplishing his wonders
through animals, not yet through specific man. But we are still in
the period when the animal was a person; and apart from that we
ourselves, whether we know it or not, need to follow also the
animal, the first thing in ourselves, to arrive at a more authoritative
statement of life and personality. There is a clear recognition of this
in a statement Christ is reported to have made in one of the earliest
gnostic documents: he tells his listeners that, if they want to enter
the Kingdom of Heaven, they must follow the fishes, the birds, and
the animals. These are the truly devout, because they do life's will,
that is God's will not their own.

Another illustration of the same truth comes from the story of
Socrates' end. When this great spirit faced the inevitable, he did
not turn to the power of reason which shone in him like a sun; he
turned to the ancient, forgotten, or neglected things in his imagination, and spent his last hours making poetry out of Aesop's fables.
His famous admonition to his friend not to forget to sacrifice a

cock to Aesculapius, which has so puzzled generations of men, seems to me a symbolic admission of hubris in his own spirit; for the cock crowing on a dungheap is an image of the spirit dedicated to pure reason, while the badge of Aesculapius was the serpent, the symbol of the instinctive in life. I see here a warning from a great human spirit that reason has a sacrifice to make to the instinct, the animal in us.

But to return to the eland. I have already mentioned that Mantis loved the eland even more than the hartebeest. One Bushman story implies this is so because Mantis made the eland first; but it also says, 'Mantis loved them not a little, he loved them dearly, for he made his heart of the eland and the hartebeest.' In some of the stories Mantis sits between the horns of the eland, in others between its toes, as if saying to the first man, 'not only my heart but also my mind and way is made of eland as well.' The reverence for the eland, which brought about its apotheosis in the Bushman spirit, emerged most impressively in the Bushman's life. His greatest paintings, dances, music, and stories were about the eland. I myself had listened many times to the Bushman singing their eland song, and found the spiritual nostalgia in it almost more than I could bear. I had watched the eland dances, seeing in their pattern the forever questing face of man, who knows how little time he has on earth to find the new vision of life he seeks. I had been told by the Bushman hunters when they killed their first eland, 'Ever since the first Bushman, we have never killed an eland for meat without saying thank you to it with a dance.'

Why did the eland play this most exalted of roles in the manifestations of their spirit? Because it is, I believe, the most civilized expression of animal life in Africa. He is a noble animal, an aristocrat. He is the greatest of the antelopes, big and strong but also extremely gentle, never using his giant strength like a giant. He is beautiful to look at, and the life within him burns like a subtle flame in the colours of his coat. Moreover, he moves through life in groups of about the same size as the Bushman did. In southern Africa it was rare to see him in vast herds, as one saw the springbuck and the gnu. It is true that after the rains he would gather near some water-filled pan, just as the scattered clans of Bushman did, and dance explosive patterns within the great community of his own kind, like the Bushman at their great gathering once a year. But before long he would be on his way again in small distinctive family groups. Then the eland has a great tenderness for his own kind. I have often watched the parent animals, resting together in the shade in the heat of the day, carry on the most intimate and delicate communion with their young, pausing from time to time to caress them with lips and tongues. Yet within this herd-expression of his life, the eland does not cease to be an individual, nor lose his fastidiousness. For instance, when the mating season comes, the eland bull takes his chosen heifer away from the herd and goes off alone with her for some days for his love-making in the bush.

From what I have seen of the eland, Mantis's choice appears to me right and inevitable: it pleases me especially to find Mantis between the eland's toes. The toes are the most sensitive part of that with which the living creature walks on earth. They are the feelers

Eland's patent-leather feet

of the ways, and the feelers of the eland are remarkably well designed for walking on desert earth. In the sands of the Kalahari his toes expand, the whole hoof becoming wider and flatter, and so prevent him from labouring too deeply in the sand. As he withdraws his black patent-leather hoof, these toes snap together with a sharp electric click. I have often lain unseen under some storm tree in the desert and listened to this wonderful sound, as the eland around me moved from one tuft of grass to another. Every time I have marvelled at this precision of the Bushman imagination that would place the spirit of transformation and regeneration which Mantis represents between such toes. For there, where the feelers of the way meet, is the centre and quick of being, the point where the impulse of the whole directs the going.

The greatest of the eland stories vary according to the storyteller and the part of southern Africa from which they come, but they all agree that the eland was a way to wisdom. In the Kalahari, for instance, Bushmen told me a beautiful story of their first spirit and the eland. They said he would wake early and wait for a sign where he lay under a tree of great wonder. First at dawn he would hear the little white, mauve, and rust-coloured dove, which has a neat black ring round its throat to show its voice is engaged to life. It would call out clear before even the dewfall was done: 'Popori! Popori! Popori! Popori!' Then far away the answer would come: 'Click! Click! Click! Click!' as the master eland strode through the bush towards the sound of the dove. The first spirit would then make for the place where both the 'Popori! Popori! Popori!' and the 'Click! Click! Click!' were going to meet. They would arrive at the same moment, the first spirit politely greeting them: 'Oh, Person of Wings I see you! Oh, Heart of Mantis, I see you.' The dove would then lead them to a place of honey, which they took out, dividing it according to their needs.

But one day the two sons of the first spirit, marvelling at the honey he brought home each day, followed him secretly and saw how he and his friends did it. They became greedy and thought they could have more honey for themselves, as well as meat, if they killed the great eland. So one day after the distribution of honey they followed the eland to his home, killed him, and ate his meat. When he did not appear the next morning, the bird and the first spirit went to look for him: they found only his bone, skin, and stomach left. Heartbroken, 'Popori' lost the power to lead the first spirit to honey, and only recovered it when the first spirit resurrected the eland out of the dung in its decaying stomach. Thereafter the eland was more masterful and beautiful than ever, helping the three of them to find even more honey than before. Out of death and corruption, greater life had come.

But why honey? Like primitive peoples the world over, Bushman had a honey mystique. Honey was not merely a physical substance but an image evoking great creative energies in his life. I have already described my encounter with the ratel in the Kalahari and told Dabé's story of the ratel and the honey-diviner. I said then that honey, in the basic imagery of man, was a symbol of wisdom. It is so with the Bushman; it is so with many other primitive peoples I know; it was so for Samson, whose riddle clearly suggested that he saw it as the sweetness which comes from the spirit who has conquered the beast, the lion himself.

Just think how impossible it is to find a substitute for honey in our current figures of speech. Try, for example, to find a substitute for honey in the phrase: 'A land of milk and honey'. 'Milk and jam' – even 'milk and strawberry jam', or any other source of sweetness – will not do. Honey it must be, because honey is the miraculous combination of light and matter, of the essences of flowers, which the bees create as food for new life when the dark hour of winter and death comes upon the world. Just as true wisdom is composed from a living awareness of the importance of innumerable small things, and of the minute advances which man's trembling spirit can achieve, so the honey comes of the tiny contributions that individual bees can make in a lifetime of service to the translucent combs in the hive. More, in making honey as food for its own new life, the bee performs a vital function for others by carrying pollen from flower to flower and fruit blossom to fruit blossom. Honey therefore represents that reciprocity at the heart of things, the understanding of which is the source of wisdom on earth.

But perhaps the point is best made by comparing the difference of role between the bee and the ant in the primal imagery of men. If the bee is a source of wisdom and creation, the ant is one of madness and distraction. Both are equally industrious and selfless, their societies are organized on similar lines; but one represents something positive in the imagination, the other something negative. I have often watched the bees tumbling among the flowers of the veld in the spring at home, and my heart has quickened at the sight. Then I have looked down at the termites hurrying through the grass around me, and shuddered at the frenzy in their movements and the mad look on their features. They destroy wherever they go; they create nothing for others.

The greatest of all Bushman stories about the eland and honey is one which was told to Bleek. It opens with Mantis starting his creation of the eland by picking up a discarded shoe of Kwammang-a, his conscious rainbow aspect. Why a shoe? The Bushman is the only person I know of among the first peoples of Africa who had evolved to the point where he made a sort of Greek sandal for himself out of the hides of animals. The shoe therefore strikes one immediately as an image of a man's way of life on earth. This to me is immensely significant. The new expression of life created despite the baboons is not final: there is also a way of life, rejected by Mantis's conscious self, which the discarded shoe of Kwam-mang-a makes him aware of.

I feel myself here in the presence of an ever-recurring mystery, which for the European has its most authoritative expression in the New Testament: 'The stone which the builders rejected is become the headstone of the corner.' Men are renewed through what they have despised and rejected, as Kwammang-a through his shoe.

So Mantis reverently takes up this piece of leather, this rejected aspect of himself, and brings it to the water where the reeds grow and the birds sing – back again to the source of first spirit in himself. He goes away: after a time he returns, and looks deeply into the water. He sees a living eland that has been formed out of the discarded leather. But he turns away, for he observes that the eland is still too small and needs the protection of the water. After what the baboons did to his young son, he is not going to repeat the mistake of sending an expression of new life into the world too soon. When he comes back the next time – miracle of miracles – he sees a small eland spoor beside the water.

I wish I could convey the excitement a man feels in Africa when, in a great empty scene without sign of living things, he suddenly comes upon a fresh spoor in the sand. The nearest equivalent in European imagination is the episode of Robinson Crusoe discovering the footprints of Man Friday on his island foreshore. Such excitement did Mantis feel. He rejoiced because the eland was strong enough to step on firm ground. The new vision, in other words, is taking shape; for creation is complete only when it becomes living behaviour, and is not fully itself till it steps out of the deep water of the imagination, the place at the centre where the reeds grow and the birds sing in us, and emerges to walk the earth in flesh and blood.

But the eland was still tiny. Mantis realized it needed help, so he went and gathered honey for it – that is, he prepared to give it wisdom as well as physical size and strength. He found the young eland standing in the water, looking shyly at him. Then suddenly the eland walked up to his father. Mantis was so moved that he wept as he fondled the young animal, and began rubbing him all over the ribs with honey. The young vision of this new way of life is being made stronger all the time with wisdom. Mantis does this several mornings running, and each visit is described by the

Bushman with love and delicacy. Then Mantis stays away from the water for three nights and for three days and nights (the magic number so closely associated with the Eleusinün and other mysteries). The eland is left to grow alone, is obviously tested by Mantis to see if it has the strength to increase itself. Here comes in the realization that the true magic in life is growth. There is no instantaneous creation of the new: even the most inspired vision needs time to grow, and if this law is not observed, only violence and disaster follows. So the eland is left to grow, and at the end of three days it is big and strong as a bull.

On the fourth day Mantis went out early. The sun rose as he walked up to the water. He called aloud: 'Kwammang-a's shoe's piece!' The eland rose up out of the water and came to him, the earth resounding as he walked. Mantis's heart filled with the greatest joy the spirit can experience – the emotion of recovering that which has been lost; of recognizing value in the despised, beauty in the ugly, and light in the shadow. This joy is expressed at one level in the Cinderella theme of so many fairy tales, and at another in the New Testament saying that the shepherd rejoices more over the return of a single lost lamb to his fold than over the presence of the many who have never strayed. As this complex emotion overflows in Mantis's heart, he sings for joy.

Ah, a person is here!
Kwammang-a's shoe's piece!
My eldest son's shoe's piece!
Kwammang-a's shoe's piece!
My eldest son's shoe's piece!

This new urge in the Bushman spirit has now found appropriate flesh and blood to live it. To use Mantis's words, it has become a person.

But the male members of Mantis's family had also become aware that he had created something new. They watched him in secret and then one day in his absence went to the water. When the eland emerged, they killed it and cut it up. The killing, here again, must not be taken in the literal sense. The first spirit of Africa is perhaps the least literal there has ever been; it is full of the ambivalence of truth. Killing and death in this ancient context mean the end of one phase and the beginning of another, the conquest and assimilation of new being. Death is the great moment of reunion and truth. In Spain to this day, when the bullfighter in the ring stands on tip-toe before the lowered horns of the bull, ready to plunge his sword into the arched neck and kill, he has a significant word for the moment. In this language of his which has come down from the archaic cult of Crete he calls it, 'the moment of truth'. Death is the supreme moment, wherein there is no room for anything but the truth, and life, shaking off what is temporary and fallible, moves on with that which has proved to be permanently true.

Here then is the importance of this killing of the first eland in Bushman mythology. Nor must the eating which followed the killing be thought of as just eating in the ordinary sense. It is eating that plays the same role in the Bushman spirit as the taking of Holy Communion does in our own. The eating of Mantis's first eland images the assimilation of new being, of a new way of life for the Bushman. This is confirmed by Mantis's reaction when he finds his special creation dead and cut up. He feels it is more than he can endure, not because the eland has been killed, but because he was not there himself to direct the killing and was unable to join in the eating; that is, he himself was not allowed to master the new being and assimilate it into his own.

After the recent joy of creation, then, he experiences the bitterest moment of all to the creator: he is separated profoundly from what he has created. He can enter into it intellectually, since his conscious rainbow aspect, Kwammang-a, joins in the killing and eating; his future self in the shape of the mongoose, Ichneumon, can experience it in full; but he, the Mantis as he is, cannot. He is a sort of insect Moses, who can lead his chosen persons of the early race to a promised land, but is not allowed to enter it himself.

Mantis watches his family carry away the eland meat; then on some pretext he goes back alone to the scene of the killing. There he finds the gall of the eland on a bush – the one part of the animal which even the Bushman could not digest. He finds there, in other words, the bitterness, the suffering which his own act of creation and his exclusion from it inflicts on him. Instinctively he knows, although he has had no previous experience, that he must come to terms with the gall of creation too. He struggles therefore with the negations of his bitterness; as the story puts it he has an argument with the gall. He tells it he will pierce it and jump on it. One way or another he will rid himself of it. The gall argues back, warning him that if he does, it will burst wide open and 'cover him in'. Mantis is tempted to evade the gall by following the children. Yet the feeling that he must accept the bitterness as his own responsibility sends him back. He pierces the gall. It bursts and, as it has warned him, covers him all over. A great blackness descended upon him – his cup of bitterness is full and running over; he gropes about in utter darkness until his fingers touch an ostrich feather. He immediately grasps at this feather of the bird of truth, which long, long ago had given him fire.

Immediately the intuition becomes clearer, the conscious will joins in the task of pursuing this intimation of the reality beyond the darkness. With the feather he wipes the gall from his forehead, face, and eyes. Had he not suffered thus, he might never have known that there was provision in the first spirit for a way through darkness and death. Recognizing this, he is freed from darkness and ready to walk in new light. As the Bushman image had it, he throws the feather up into the sky and with a lift of heart speaks to it as follows: 'You must now lie up in the sky, you must henceforth be the moon. You shall shine at night. You shall by your shining lighten the darkness for men, till the sun rises to light up all things for man. It is he under whom men hunt. You glow for man, while the sun shines for man. Under him men walk about, they go hunting, they return home. You are the moon, you give light to men, then you fall away, you return to life again, you give light to all the people.'

18 'Light to all the People'

The moon is the symbol of renewal in the imagination of the Bushman. It represents the intuitive elements of the spirit which carries life through the darknesses that from time to time close upon it. The sun represents the great light of day, the immense power of reason; the moon the light provided for when reason is not enough, when all our bright conscious experience fails us. In the Upanishads there is a story about Yajnavalkya, the sage at a king's court. The king asked him one day, 'By what light do human beings go out, do their work, and return?' The sage answered, 'By the light of the sun.' The king then asked, 'But when the light of the sun is extinguished, by what light do human beings go out, do they work, and return?' The sage said, 'By the light of the moon.' And so question and answer went on. When the moon is extinguished, man works by the light of the stars; when they are quenched, by the light of fire. And when the light of the fire itself is put out, the king asked: 'By what light then can they do their work and still live?' The sage replied: 'By the light of the self.'

I think also of one legend of Buddha's death. When he was dying the animals of the earth crowded round him, weeping bitterly. 'Do not weep,' he comforted them, as the moon in the Bushman story once tried to comfort the people of the early race. 'Look at the moon!' he said: 'as the moon dying renews herself again, so shall I dying be renewed again.'

So there then we have two great stages of man in the saga of Mantis: the recognition that life has a meaning only through creation beyond its immediate self, as in the story of young Mantis and the baboons; the second, that this act of creation must be in the context also of a community on earth as reflected in the life and character of the eland. There is a third now: the importance of living life on earth within the community as an individual. The story that describes this challenge to the Bushman spirit most clearly, significantly makes no mention of Mantis, as if implying that this is a part of creation man must take upon himself alone. Yet I shall include it here because Mantis made it possible for the Bushman spirit to arrive at this new stage in life. The story is called 'The Young Man and the Lion.'

One day, so the Bushman told Bleek, a young man of the early race went out hunting. He climbed a hill to look about for game, and there to his surprise began to feel sleepy. He should have been warned by that: it was a notorious axiom among the first people that animals defended themselves against hunters by inducing sleep in them. A little animal induced a little sleep, a dangerous animal a great sleep. Even to this day in the Kalahari the Bushman believes it, and this young man of the early race should have known that such a desire to sleep in the light of day could only have been caused by one of the greatest of animals. To give the image its modern idiom: the tendency to sleep represents the tendency to unawareness; our animal nature defends itself against the bows and arrows of the conscious mind by bringing darkness and unawareness to our spirit. It is through unawareness that fate works its will on men; the sin of Oedipus and all its tragic consequences stemmed from the son's and mother's ignorance of their true relationship to each other. So, when this young man is overcome by sleepiness it is not surprising that a lion appears.

The lion, the Bushman said, was on the way to the water because it was thirsty. Here again we meet a basic image that has recurred often in the saga, and recurs in the Bible too. Many of the parables and miracles in the New Testament are concerned with water, for a definite reason; this Bushman story uses it for a similar end: the lion too is in search of the spirit without which it cannot live; even a lion cannot live by meat alone. Why the lion? Other animals, because of some particular speciality, can claim to represent particular features of natural life; but none represents all its features as does the lion. Its beauty and power in the animal world are those of balance and proportion. An elephant has as fine a nose, as good a hearing, and greater stature, but his sight is extremely poor. There is something over-specialized or lacking in every candidate for the throne. Only the lion has all the qualities – the sight, the scent, the hearing, the intelligence, the courage, the speed, and the strength. Moreover the lion is as much at home in the night as it is in the day; and above all it is an individual. The phrase 'the cat that walks alone' was not idly coined. One reason why the

'The lion . . . was on his way to the water'

lion is so dangerous is precisely that it is an individual. The experience of the great hunters of Africa, and to a much lesser extent my own, has taught me how dangerous it is to generalize about the species. You have to know your lion individually before you dare predict what it might do; and even then, so much has it a mind of its own, you are often wrong. This lion, therefore, represents what is animal, natural, in the most individual sense.

No sooner does it see the sleeping man than it goes silently over to him and takes him. When the young man awakes he is already being dragged towards a tree. Afraid that if he stirs the lion may kill him, he keeps still, pretending to be dead. The lion places him in the fork of a black storm tree – a tree which has no thorns and bears lovely yellow flowers. There a great conflict takes place within the lion: shall it eat the young man first and then drink, or drink first and then eat? The lion's sense of first-things-first decides the issue: it will go to the water before it eats – will begin with the spirit before it starts with the flesh. So, fixing the young man still more firmly into the fork of the tree, it sets out towards the water. But on the way its doubts return; it looks constantly over its shoulder to make certain the young man has not moved.

At last the lion is over the hill – has, as it were, surmounted the doubt of its own vision: yet it is compelled to return for one last look. It thinks the young man may have moved, because it has perhaps not fixed him securely enough in the tree of life. Through half-open eyelids the young man sees the lion approach. He knows he is in great danger and must keep still; but the lion has fixed him so firmly in the fork of the tree that a sharp bit of wood protrudes into his back, hurting him intensely. Already he has been crying quietly to himself, and the tears have started to run down his cheek. When the lion reaches him, it immediately sees the tears and gently licks them away. Now the situation alters. Because of the tears, life can never be the same again for the young man or the lion. After tasting the tears, after sharing the suffering of the young man, the lion is linked for good or ill to this hunter and no one else. It is an instance of the dynamic element of compassion asserting itself in the first spirit of things. Though the lion disappears over the hill to drink the life-giving water, we know that, whatever happens, it will return.

The moment the young man is convinced the lion has gone for a while, he jumps up and runs back to his own community. He runs in a tremendous zigzag, because he knows that, since the lion has licked away his tears, it will come after him. He does all he can to put this lion of heaven off the scent – to evade or at least postpone the reckoning which compassion demands between him and his own royal individual nature. He tells his people that there is a lion coming after him. He begs them to wrap him up tightly in as many of the tough skins of Mantis's beloved hartebeest as they possess: in other words, he tries to take refuge in the attitude of the community to nature. The community tries to oblige because, the Bushman says, 'He was a young man the hearts of the people loved dearly.'

Before long the lion arrives, looking for the young man. The whole community rallies to destroy it with spears and arrows. They attack it for many hours, but the lion appears indestructible. It only says, again and again, 'I have come for the young man whose tears I have licked and whom I must find.' The people offer the lion young children and even a girl instead, but the lion refuses to be side-tracked. Towards night-fall the frightened community realizes not only that it cannot interfere, but also that if it goes on it will be endangered: the reckoning, at this royal level, must be between individuals – the lion and the young hunter. Despite his mother's pleading, they take the young man out of his protective covering and give him to the lion. The lion recognizes him, kills him, and speaks to the people for the last time, saying that now it has found him whom it sought, the moment has come when the people may kill it. With these words the lion lies down and dies beside the man whose tears it has licked.

Remembering what the image of death meant to the Bushman, it is clear for me that the animal in the individual and the individual in the animal have been mastered, so that they can be united and re-created, in the imagination of the Bushman, as something greater than either. It is as if the creative pattern of the first spirit was saying to stone-age man, 'There must be between you and life a reconciliation which the community cannot make for you. There are matters wherein you cannot hide for ever behind the attitude of the community without imperilling both the community and yourself. Nature demands in its supreme expression that it should be lived individually. You must not, therefore, fall asleep on the way to the water of life. Keep your eyes open, know yourself, and so go out to meet your own royal nature in order to become an individual and fear-free man.'

We come now to the fourth and last stage of Mantis's life on earth. It is the story of stories and, fittingly enough, the last great Bushman story told. The time is later than the Bushman knows – later even than his soul, Porcupine, thinks. In the world without, his enemies are closing in on him fast for the kill. We know this because for the first time the sheep – the animal furthest removed from his natural associates and most dependent on the will of civilized man – appears in a Bushman story. In a legend that immediately precedes this one, there is already a feeling as of a twilight of the gods: doom sags darkly over the great scene from which the first actor of life is being driven by black and white men. Mantis himself has been badly beaten by the owners of sheep, the black men who are, he says, as numerous and as thirsty for blood as the ticks in the fleeces of the sheep. He has escaped only by taking refuge for the last time in his natural spirit, his magic cloak of hartebeest skin. Hurt in spirit, aching in body, he reaches home and curses those who have hurt him. He foretells how, because of what men have done to him, they shall forfeit the fire of life; forfeit the sheep, the civilization and culture of which the sheep is the symbol, and like ticks be condemned to live on uncooked food and raw blood. Who can say that the prophecy is not being fulfilled in my country, for both the black and white who so ruthlessly exterminated Mantis's Bushman children?

However, Mantis would not be Mantis if he arrested himself in curses and prophecies. He realizes that there is something wrong in himself also or all this could not have happened to him. He knows that, unless he puts himself right, all life is doomed. After the realization of creation beyond the brittle moment, after creation through sweet society of men, after the creation of individual man creating alone out of his loneliness like the great spirit at the beginning, there comes this greatest of all acts of creation: the first spirit, the god, must renew himself too. And it is true that in the twilight hour, if the night is not to fall again for ever, man must renew himself by renewing his relationship with his God – must let the divine first image renew itself through him. That the supreme being is involved is clear, for me, from the fact that for the first time all the dearest and closest elements of Mantis are committed to the battle.

When he declares himself to be inadequate, by announcing in the ancient way that he is extremely unwell, he does so to the full assembly of all the delegates of the vital aspects of himself. Kaura, the dassie, his wife, the uncompromising social realist, charged with the thankless task of keeping his winged feet on earth, is there.

Porcupine: the love of Mantis's life

So is Kwammang-a, his fine, discriminating rainbow element: so too Kwammang-a's sons – Ichneumon the mongoose, the enterprising future self of Mantis, volubly articulate with the meaning which Mantis himself could only live, and the young Kwammang-a, quiet, resolute and brave, ready to act out an even further aspect of the Mantis. There also is their mother, Porcupine, Mantis's soul and daughter, his lady of the starry sky of Africa. Before them all, Mantis confesses his inadequacy.

All sorts of little things tell us how deep is the sense of crisis in Mantis's assembly. Porcupine, the prophetic soul, feels it most. She knows, as no one else does, that moments of renewal are also moments of extreme peril. Just before Mantis speaks, we are shown how tense her own spirit is. She calls her husband, the rain-bow element, Kwammang-a, and for the first time she uses her own feminine diminutive of endearment for him. She cries with awe and alarm, 'Oh! *Kwa*! Look at the sheep standing here which Mantis has brought.' She has never addressed him before except by the formal title of Kwammang-a with which all Bushmen saluted the appearance of the rainbow.

It makes me think of times in the war when danger brought out in just such a way men's yearning to be 'members one of another'. I recall one instance specially when my commanding officer, a most controlled and reticent man, had to order a soldier to do something which meant almost certain death. He called him then, not by his surname as he had always done so punctiliously, not even by his Christian name or his nickname of 'Ginger', which no one even suspected that the C.O. knew; he called him 'Gin', as only his most intimate friends did, and in the tone of voice in which I imagine Porcupine speaking to her husband *Kwa*.

In that atmosphere of gathering stress, they hear Mantis say, 'I am writhing with pain. Before I can cut up this sheep for us to eat, this swelling must disappear.' His being unable to eat implies that the swelling is also in his throat. Now it is interesting here that in the Indian Chakras the throat was a sort of *logos* region where, according to the Tantric text, a personality who attains a certain level of evolution is given the power of the word, of meaning, and so becomes a truly wise person. This might indicate that Mantis's sickness means he is having grave trouble in finding the right word, the true concept for the re-statement of life and personality which the perilous situation demands. The impression is strengthened by Mantis's remark a little later: 'I can talk then, for I do not talk now.'

Yet, full as Mantis's house is, the assembly is not complete: one great character is missing – the All-Devourer. For the first time now he is to be summoned. Hitherto transformation and re-transformation, birth and rebirth, have been accomplished by Mantis through his own various aspects, but now even they are not enough. Mantis says to Porcupine: 'You must go to your father, the All-Devourer, that he may help me eat up these sheep . . . I feel my heart is upset, so I want the Old Man yonder to come . . . and I can talk then, for I do not talk now.' The 'Old Man yonder', a new name for the All-Devourer, is the first indication that he is some far aspect of Mantis – how dread an aspect, we shall soon see. As the man yonder is Porcupine's father, from whom she fled to find refuge with Mantis, she is horrified. She tries desperately to dissuade Mantis. But Mantis will not listen. He insists that all the sheep should be assembled for the All-Devourer to eat on his arrival.

It is significant that it is sheep Mantis assembles. Sheep of all animals in the world express two things: the natural subject of civilization and culture, and the quality of acceptance, of bowing to necessity. Anyone who has killed as many sheep as I have will know this last quality well. Even when the knife is at its throat the sheep does not struggle: it makes no sound while its throat is being cut. It accepts death as no other animal on earth. What Mantis affirms by the assembly of sheep is that only in complete acceptance of the necessity of the All-Devourer can any good be gained from the situation. Like Job, he is prepared to resign himself to fate, however unfair it may be. Besides, the All-Devourer will eat with him the meat of acceptance. Freely the whole of life – or, as a modern psychologist might put it, both the conscious and the unconscious in Mantis – will accept what is and what is to come. There can be no more evasion.

This is made clearer still by Mantis's refusal to eat any more zebra meat. That meat, he says, is white with age; in other words the zebra's way is old stuff, has been tried before and found wanting. The zebra is the animal of evasion and gipsy-like movement across the great plains; the creature without roots. Few African peoples to this day will eat it, so afraid are they of becoming like it. No more of it for Mantis either: bravely he says, 'no more flight'. After all Porcupine's pleas have failed, she says sadly: 'Nevertheless, I will fetch him [the All-Devourer] tomorrow, that he may come, then you will see him for yourself with your own eyes.'

Yet, being wise in the ways of the prophetic soul, she tells her son to take some meat and hide it so that neither Mantis nor the All-Devourer can find it. She knows what to extract of truth in the situation, and put safely aside, so that after the disaster the new young life shall have some true nourishment with which to begin.

Porcupine then sets out to find the All-Devourer and tells him: 'Mantis, your cousin yonder, invites you to come and help eat up the sheep, for his heart is troubling him.' She returns quickly and Mantis asks: 'Where is your father?' She answers: 'He is still on the way.' Then she commands Mantis: 'Look at the bush standing up above, to see if a shadow comes gliding from above. Watch for the bush to break off. Then you shall look out for the shadow when you see that the bushes up there have disappeared. For his tongue will take away the bushes beforehand while he is still approaching behind the hill. Then his body will come up and the bushes round us will be devoured. We shall no longer sit hidden.'

Having delivered her warning, she sees to it that her son eats meat in plenty, thereby making him strong for the part he has to play.

There comes then a most moving description of how in this great empty wasteland Mantis, the tiny insect figure of Being, the aspect of the first spirit, sits waiting, while the All-Devourer approaches, consuming everything on the way, breathing fire in Porcupine's spoor. Through that which separated itself from him in the beginning, he is being led back to a fateful reunion. Suddenly a great shadow falls on Mantis. He cries to his soul, his daughter: 'Why is it so dark when there are no clouds in the sky?' It seems that the heroic God momentarily shrinks back from the end he himself has willed in order to be renewed. Because of that hesitation, the darkness becomes greater than ever. It is the moment of Job on his ash heap, and a far, far precursor of a greater forsaken moment on the Cross. It is also the moment for my own generation when the All-Devourer has twice been summoned in world wars to overcome the inadequate in the spirit of man. Here is a contemporary poet's idea of a predicament similar to that in which Mantis found himself:

> Between the idea
> And the reality
> Between the motion
> And the act
> Falls the shadow.

229

Between the conception
And the creation
Between the emotion
And the response
Falls the shadow.

Between the desire
And the spasm
Between the potency
And the existence
Between the essence
And the descent
Falls the shadow.

In the heart of the shadow Mantis sees the fire, that is the tongue of the 'Man yonder', consuming all. Then the dread moment is upon him: he has to sit down and eat with the All-Devourer. The supper is described at great length. In the end Mantis, all the sheep, all his shelters and worldly belongings are eaten; even his rainbow element is swallowed up.

As Kwammang-a vanishes into the vast stomach stretching from horizon to horizon, Porcupine weeps. Then her courage returns, for she has her two sons – Mantis's and Kwammang-a's future selves – with her still. She turns against her terrible father without hesitation as Ariadne turned against hers in the story of the Minotaur. Taking the two boys apart, she tests them with the point of a spear made red-hot in the fire. Why a spear? Because it is an image of man's conscious will. She presses the red-hot metal on their temples to test their intelligence, their response to her heroic intuition. She pushes the burning spear into their ears to try their understanding. She tests them even by pushing the glowing point into their nostrils to see if their intuition, their vision of the future, matches her own. The one boy's eyes fill with tears, and she says: 'A mild person is one for whom tears gather.' Yet she does not despise tears – who should know better than she that even in the dark hour compassion too has its own vital role to play if another form of excess is not to be born? As she tests the young Kwammang-a, to her delight the brave, the quiet one does not fail. The moment for his special qualities has come. The deeper she burns him with the spear, the drier his eyes become – in other words, the clearer the vision he achieves. She exclaims with profound exultation at last: 'Yes, a fierce man is this, he resembles his father.'

Warning them that the All-Devourer's tongue is a terrible fire, she sends out the two to do their work. The mild, the compassionate one, because he cuts with his left hand, is seated on the left of the All-Devourer, on the side called sinister, matching instinct against instinct. The fierce one, being right-handed, is seated on the right, matching the will against the will. Between them they rip open the All-Devourer's belly and deliver Mantis and his rainbow element; bushes, shelters, sheep, the whole world that has been eaten, tumble out next with such a rush that the boys have to jump aside.

Thereafter Porcupine sees to it that Dassie, the realist, gives Mantis water while she looks after her own husband. How things have changed as a result of the disaster is clear even in this tiny detail. Hitherto Dassie in her earth-bound will has had to curb Mantis's spirit; but now she has become capable of encouraging it, for this is what the giving of water means here. Meanwhile Porcupine prepares some of the food of the truth, some of the being she put by before the disaster, and gives it to them all to eat. Then, making them gather their belongings, she takes full charge, saying: 'We will go away. We will go far away and leave the All-Devourer lying outside this hut.' With these words she leads them away to a new home and a new country, which means, in the language of first things, to a new state of being.

There, for me, the story of Mantis is complete. Whether the Bushman would have added another stage to it, had he lived, no one can say for certain: after the slaying of the All-Devourer, the rest is silence. We know only that the vanished story-teller said that Mantis and his family, at their new home in their new state of being, lived in peace. That may have been wishful thought of one who had known peace but was never to know it again; or it may have been, as I am inclined to believe, his way of saying there is no more to be said. Other people at other times have re-stated the theme in other words; but the Bushman imagination took this theme as far as any men have been able to take it in terms comprehensible to our limited understanding. What lies ahead of the human spirit can only be reached through the slow process of living our way towards it, as Mantis and his own lived theirs.

But we can at least know that there is a pattern in us, communicated through images that came like star-light into our spirit, and that by serving them with all our heart and mind, life on earth can become richer, freer, and greater than it has ever been. This pattern is not limited to 'birth, copulation, death'. It is one of birth, pro-creation, death, and rebirth. These four are the gateways to a great city; they are four angelic elements implicit in every moment of life lived freely in obedience to the great pattern. All together, they make of life, not a dead-end valley, but an eternal *here* and *now*.

Let the last word be with the Bushman. As the story of Dxui began with fire – fire that separated the first spirit of creation from its own begetter, and as Mantis was the bringer of the fire, so let me come to the end with fire. The circle rounds. There was fire at the beginning of the Bushman story; there is fire at its end. The wood burns out, the ashes in the desert are scattered. But the fire itself burns on. The knowledge which separated stone-age man from God, the father in his first spirit, and drove him to the mountain tops, at the moment when flesh and blood crumble on earth, this very awareness, this fire re-unites him with God. When a Bushman in the Kalahari dies, he is buried deep in the red sand in his blanket of hartebeest skin, face to the East, with his bow and quiver full of arrows, his spear at hand, and beside him an ostrich egg full of water for the long journey. Then, crying bitterly, his companions pile the wood high at the foot of the grave and light a great fire.

When I asked the reason for this, they said: 'But don't you know it is dark where he is at present? He has far to go and needs the light of the fire to take him to the day beyond.'

So the fire is there always, the flame clean and clear on the last horizon like the blade of the spear that delivered Mantis from the All-Devourer. And always too there is the moon, this feather of the bird of truth that gave the fire to man. One night in the Kalahari, when the sky was clear and the moon rose full, the Bushmen began dancing. They danced so long and with such a passion that I knew it was no ordinary dance. I asked my favourite hunter: 'Why do you dance on and on like this?' He looked at me, amazed, and said: 'From now on the moon will begin to fade away, and unless we show the moon that our hearts love its light not a little, it will fade utterly away and not come back but altogether die.'

All this became for me, on my long journey home by sea, an image of what is wanted in the spirit of man today. We live in a sunset hour of time. We need to recognize and develop that aspect of ourselves of which the moon bears the image. It is our own shy intuitions of renewal, which walk in our spiritual night as Porcupine walked by the light of the moon, that need helping on the way. It is as if I hear the wind bringing up behind me the voice of Mantis, the infinite in the small, calling from the stone age to an age of men with hearts of stone, commanding us with the authentic voice of eternal renewal: 'You must henceforth be the moon. You must shine at night. By your shining shall you lighten the darkness until the sun rises again to light up all things for men.'

' His fingers touched a falling feather '

Penguinews *and* Penguins in Print

Every month we issue an illustrated magazine, *Penguinews*. It's a lively guide to all the latest Penguins, Pelicans and Puffins, and always contains an article on a major Penguin author, plus other features of contemporary interest.

Penguinews is supplemented by *Penguins in Print*, a complete list of all the available Penguin titles – there are now over four thousand!

Why not write for a free copy of this month's *Penguinews*? And if you'd like both publications sent for a year, just send us a cheque or a postal order for 30p (if you live in the United Kingdom) or 60p (if you live elsewhere), and we'll put you on our mailing list.

Dept EP, Penguin Books Ltd,
Harmondsworth, Middlesex

Note: *Penguinews* and *Penguins in Print* are not available in the U.S.A. or Canada

The Lost World of the Kalahari
Laurens van der Post

In this enthralling book a distinguished explorer
and writer describes his rediscovery of the Bushmen,
outcast survivors from Stone Age Africa. Laurens
van der Post was fascinated and appalled at the fate
of this remarkable people, who seemed to him a
reminder of our own 'legitimate beginnings'.

Attacked by all the races that came after them in
Africa, the last of the Bushmen have in modern
times been driven deep into the Kalahari Desert. It
was there, in the scorching heat of an African August,
that Colonel van der Post led his famous expedition.
His search for these small, hardy aboriginals, with
their physical peculiarities, their cave art, and their
music-making, provides the author with material for
a dramatic and compassionate book.

'He is even better in print than he was on TV' –
J. B. Priestley in *Reynolds News*

'No one can write more feelingly of Africa . . . an
experience not to be missed' – Elspeth Huxley in the
Evening Standard

Not for sale in the U.S.A.

Laurens van der Post

Journey into Russia

'The next best thing to seeing the place for oneself . . .
is to read *Journey into Russia* . . . sceptical, well-informed,
unprejudiced and amusing. A truly civilized, discriminating
observer' – *Guardian*

'He went to Russia for the first time in 1961 with an open
mind; he travelled all over the Soviet Union in four
separate journeys, and spoke to thousands of people,
from almost every walk of life. . . . As a general picture of
Russia today there can hardly be a better book' –
Listener

'An honest account . . . full of delightful vignettes of
Soviet life brought out with a subtle sense of humour' –
Daily Worker

Not for sale in the U.S.A.

The White Nile
Alan Moorehead

In reviewing *The White Nile* in the *Observer* Sir
Harold Nicolson spoke of the gigantic ghosts that
haunt the Sudan. They are ghosts of many
nationalities: the Khedive Ismail, the Mahdi, savage
King Mutesa of Buganda, and a bevy of Arab
slave traders. There is Richard Burton, the restless,
inscrutable scholar; his dull but vindicated opponent,
Speke; Livingstone, the indomitable Scot; Baker and
his beautiful Hungarian wife; the bumptious American
journalist, Stanley, who searched for Livingstone and
later for the German scientist, Emin Pasha. And
finally there is Gordon, the strange, heroic martyr of
Khartoum.

These, in their full stature, Alan Moorehead parades
before us in this account of the opening of the Nile.
It is a story which enforces respect for the Victorians'
faith in civilization and their hatred of slavery.

'He appears to have visited every inch of the scene
himself and puts it before us with simplicity and
power' – V. S. Pritchett in the *New Statesman*

Also available:
THE FATAL IMPACT
NO ROOM IN THE ARK

Not for sale in the U.S.A.

Venture to the Interior

Laurens van der Post

This is the story of a journey made in 1949, at the request of the British Government, to investigate little-known territory in Nyasaland, the remote Mlanje, and the inaccessible Nyika plateau. Laurens van der Post brilliantly evokes for us such events as a charge of zebras, an auction of Victorian furnishings in the heart of Africa, the psychological effects of an African drum, or the catastrophe which befell his party on Mount Mlanje.

'The reflective passages are very important and the idea of framing them in the journeys is inspired, and some of the poetic descriptions of the scenery are most beautiful and fill me with envy. I think the book is magnificent' – Stephen Spender

Also available
Flamingo Feather
The Seed and the Sower
The Hunter and the Whale

Not for sale in the U.S.A.